Vantage Point

Enhancing Communication Skills through High-Interest Topics

Eric Hirata

NATIONAL
GEOGRAPHIC
LEARNING

JN125066

Australia · Brazil · Mexico · Singapore · United Kingdom · United States

Vantage Point—Enhancing Communication Skills through High-Interest Topics

Eric Hirata

© 2023 Cengage Learning K.K.

ISBN: 978-4-86312-403-5

National Geographic Learning | Cengage Learning K.K.
No. 2 Funato Building 5th Floor
1-11-11 Kudankita, Chiyoda-ku
Tokyo 102-0073
Japan

Tel: 03-3511-4392
Fax: 03-3511-4391

Preface

As globalization continues to spread into every industry and aspect of our daily lives, the need to understand global issues has become increasingly important. With borders shrinking and cultures blending, we should understand that many of the issues that we face are universal and need to be discussed to help eliminate or minimize them in the future. On an everyday basis, the food we eat, sports we follow, technology we use, people we work with, and news we read about are represented by a mixture of nationalities and cultures. In other words, almost everything we do is a global matter.

Vantage Point is a content-based English textbook that considers a variety of different matters, or issues, which are relevant to our lives. The activities in this textbook will help you develop your English skills as well as your overall knowledge of various issues around the world by focusing on "learning *in* English" rather than just "learning English."

The main aim of this textbook is to improve your English communication skills through numerous discussion activities about global issues. The organization of each unit is scaffolded to build up your knowledge of the content as you progress through the activities. The reading and listening activities give you plenty of input on the topic of each unit while the discussion and writing tasks provide you with output opportunities to improve your English skills.

Regardless of where you live, you have been and will continue to be affected by other cultures and countries. The next time you are in your Japanese-made car, drinking your Italian coffee or British tea, while listening to music on your American-made phone, take a moment to consider the influence countries have on one another. Then, have fun learning about the global matters that are presented in this textbook and broaden your vantage point on how you see the world.

Eric Hirata

Table of Contents

Overview

This textbook covers five themes. Each theme consists of an Introduction, three units comprised of eight sections, and a Wrap-Up described below:

Introduction

Presents the three units. The quotations show opinions about the topics of the units. You can talk with your classmates about these quotations and get an idea of what you will be studying.

Vocabulary

Introduces the five keywords from the passage in the Reading section. These words come from the Academic Word List and often appear in English academic texts. Learning these keywords will help you discuss the topic of the unit and understand the content of the passage.

Warm-Up

Helps activate what you already know about some contents in the unit. In Part A, by giving your ideas and opinions about the pictures and questions, you can practice language that will be useful for the unit. In Part B, the eight statements ask you to agree or disagree with issues related to the topic of the unit. By giving reasons for your opinions, you can build your communication skills.

Listening [1]

Provides authentic listening input. The conversation previews some of the content that will appear later in the unit. Parts A and B check your listening comprehension. Part C has discussion questions about the information in the conversation.

Pre-Reading

Gives you a chance to consider some ideas and issues that will be mentioned in the passage of the Reading section. You can develop a deeper perspective by sharing opinions with your classmates.

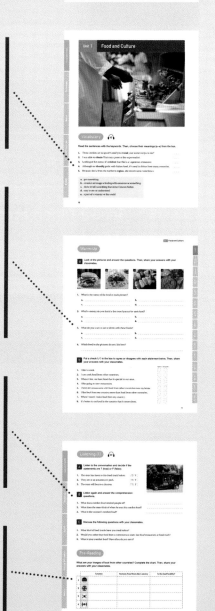

Reading

Provides content input for the unit. In Part A, the passage explores important ideas and issues related to the topic of the unit. By using examples from authentic sources, the passage gives real world news events and experiences to help connect the reading to everyday life. Part B has discussion questions about the information in the passage.

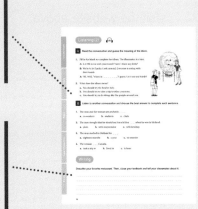

Listening [2]

Deepens your understanding of the content of the unit. Part A introduces an idiom with a visual aid and a short conversation of the idiom in use. Part B provides a new conversation and checks your listening comprehension.

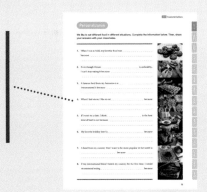

Writing

Asks you to describe your experience or what you would do in a situation relating to the topic of the unit. This activity allows you the chance to develop writing skills and encourages you to utilize all that you have learned in the unit.

Personalization

Encourages you to consider the contents of the unit from a personal standpoint. The activity completes the unit with practical questions and examples that invite you to share your own experiences and opinions with your classmates.

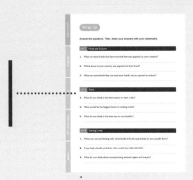

Wrap-Up

Reviews the topics of the three units. Three questions per unit ask you to recall the knowledge from the unit and apply it to these discussion questions.

How to Access the Audio Online

For activities with a headset icon ( ), the audio is available at the website below.

https://ngljapan.com/vtgpt-audio/

You can access the audio as outlined below.

1 Visit the website above.

2 Click the link to the content you would like to listen to.

Alternatively, scan the QR code with a smartphone or tablet to visit the website above.

Food and Health

Food is an important part of our lives and what we eat relates to our health.
How does the food we eat influence our health?

Unit 1 Food and Culture

"One cannot think well, love well, sleep well, if one has not dined well."
Virginia Woolf

Unit 2 Diets

"Once you have to start counting calories, it takes away from the joy of eating."
Mireille Guiliano

Unit 3 Saving Lives

"Part of the secret of success in life is to eat what you like and let the food fight it out inside."
Mark Twain

Unit 1   Food and Culture

Vocabulary

Read the sentences with the keywords. Then, choose their meanings (a–e) from the box.

1. These cookies are so good! Could you **reveal** your secret recipe to me? _____

2. I was able to **obtain** Thai curry paste at the supermarket. _____

3. Looking at the menu, it's **evident** that this is a vegetarian restaurant. _____

4. Although we **identify** garlic with Italian food, it's used in dishes from many countries. _____

5. Because she is from the northern **region**, she misses snow sometimes. _____

> **a.** get something
> **b.** connect an image or feeling with someone or something
> **c.** show or tell something that wasn't known before
> **d.** easy to see or understand
> **e.** a part of a country or the world

Warm-Up

A Look at the pictures and answer the questions. Then, share your answers with your classmates.

a   b   c   d

1. What is the name of the food in each picture?

   a. _____   b. _____

   c. _____   d. _____

2. Which country do you think is the most famous for each food?

   a. _____   b. _____

   c. _____   d. _____

3. What do you want to eat or drink with these foods?

   a. _____   b. _____

   c. _____   d. _____

4. Which food in the pictures do you like best?

   _____

B Put a check (✓) in the box to agree or disagree with each statement below. Then, share your answers with your classmates.

	Agree	Disagree
1. I like to cook.	☐	☐
2. I can cook food from other countries.	☐	☐
3. Where I live, we have food that is special to our area.	☐	☐
4. I like going to new restaurants.	☐	☐
5. There are restaurants with food from other countries near my home.	☐	☐
6. I like food from my country more than food from other countries.	☐	☐
7. When I travel, I miss food from my country.	☐	☐
8. It's better to eat food in the country that it comes from.	☐	☐

Unit 1   Unit 2   Unit 3   Unit 4   Unit 5   Unit 6   Unit 7   Unit 8   Unit 9   Unit 10   Unit 11   Unit 12   Unit 13   Unit 14   Unit 15

Listening [1] 03

A Listen to the conversation and decide if the statements are T (true) or F (false).

1. The man has been to this food truck before. [T / F]
2. They are at an amusement park. [T / F]
3. The man will buy two churros. [T / F]

B Listen again and answer the comprehension questions.

1. What does comfort food remind people of? _____
2. What does the man think of when he eats his comfort food? _____
3. What is the woman's comfort food? _____

C Discuss the following questions with your classmates.

1. What kind of food trucks have you tried before?
2. Would you rather buy food from a convenience store, fast food restaurant, or food truck?
3. What is your comfort food? How often do you eat it?

Pre-Reading

What are your images of food from other countries? Complete the chart. Then, share your answers with your classmates.

		Country	Famous Food from the Country	Is the food healthy?
1				
2				
3				
4				

Reading 04

A Read the passage and answer the comprehension questions.

The kind of food you eat can **reveal** where you are from. In the past, Japan got most of its food from the ocean and land as people grew rice and vegetables. However, the US is a much bigger country, so many people do not live near an ocean. As a result, early in US history, people **obtained** food through hunting. The history of both countries is **evident** in the food that is often **identified** with each country—seafood with Japan and meat with the US.

In some countries, fishing is an important part of the culture.

Even within a country, food can be different. In Japan, many different **regions** have their own kind of ramen. While many people eat *tonkotsu* ramen in Fukuoka, *miso* ramen is often eaten in Sapporo. In the US, the kind of hot dog a person likes can show where the person is from. A Chicago dog with tomatoes, onions, pickles, peppers, mustard, and relish is much different from a slaw dog—a hot dog with coleslaw in the southern part of the US.

California rolls come from Western culture.

Culture can also change food. For example, people around the world started to try sushi more because of California rolls. Since California rolls have avocado and crab meat instead of raw fish, people wanted to try them. As more people began to like them, they started to try other sushi as well. Now, there are many sushi restaurants around the world. Each country has a different history with food. As countries become more global, food culture will continue to grow as well.

....

1. Where did Japan get most of its food from in the past?

   _____

2. Which food do people often identify with the US?

   _____

3. Why did people want to try California rolls?

   _____

B Discuss the following questions with your classmates.

1. Which do you prefer to eat, seafood or meat?

2. What are some foods from your country that people around the world know?

3. What are some other foods that are served differently in other countries?

Listening [2] 05

A Read the conversation and guess the meaning of the idiom.

1. Fill in the blank to complete the idiom. The illustration is a hint.

    A: Is it OK to eat with your hands? Aren't there any forks?

    B: We're in Sri Lanka. Look around. Everyone is eating with their hands.

    A: OK. Well, "when in _____," I guess. Let's use our hands!

2. What does the idiom mean?

    a. You should try the food in Italy.

    b. You should try to take a trip to other countries.

    c. You should try to do things like the people around you.

B Listen to another conversation and choose the best answer to complete each sentence.

1. The man and the woman are probably _____.

    a. co-workers   **b.** students   **c.** chefs

2. The man thought that he should eat French fries _____ when he was in Holland.

    a. plain   **b.** with mayonnaise   **c.** with ketchup

3. The man studied in Holland for _____.

    a. eighteen months   **b.** a year   **c.** six months

4. The woman _____ Canada.

    a. took a trip to   **b.** lived in   **c.** is from

Writing

Describe your favorite restaurant. Then, close your textbook and tell your classmates about it.

_____

_____

_____

_____

_____

Personalization

We like to eat different food in different situations. Complete the information below. Then, share your answers with your classmates.

1. When I was a child, my favorite food was _____

   because _____

   _____ .

2. Even though I know _____ is unhealthy,

   I can't stop eating it because _____

   _____ .

3. A famous food from my hometown is _____ .

   I recommend it because _____

   _____ .

4. When I feel stress, I like to eat _____ because

   _____

   _____ .

5. If I went on a date, I think _____ is the best

   kind of food to eat because _____

   _____ .

6. My favorite holiday food is _____ because

   _____

   _____ .

7. A food from my country that I want to be more popular in the world is

   _____ because _____

   _____ .

8. If my international friend visited my country for the first time, I would

   recommend eating _____ because

   _____ .

Unit 2   Diets

Vocabulary   06

Read the sentences with the keywords. Then, choose their meanings (a–e) from the box.

1. I'm not that hungry, so I'll just have a small **portion** of cake. _____

2. I got over my **depression** of failing the test by eating ice cream every day for two weeks. _____

3. Losing weight is a **benefit** of getting lots of exercise. _____

4. A main **factor** in staying healthy is not to eat so many snacks between meals. _____

5. The fitness **expert** said taking short walks during the day is good for my mental health. _____

  a. a good point about something
  b. a very sad feeling over a length of time
  c. something that can change a situation for good or for bad
  d. someone who has a lot of skill or information about something
  e. a part of something

Warm-Up

A Look at the pictures and answer the questions. Then, share your answers with your classmates.

a 500 ml bottle

a medium slice

a small bowl

a small cone

1. How many calories do you think are in the food or drink?

   a. _____   b. _____

   c. _____   d. _____

2. How often do you have them?

   a. _____   b. _____

   c. _____   d. _____

3. Where do you usually have them?

   a. _____   b. _____

   c. _____   d. _____

4. How has your diet changed since you were a child?

   _____

B Put a check (✓) in the box to agree or disagree with each statement below. Then, share your answers with your classmates.

	Agree	Disagree
1. I think I'm healthy.	☐	☐
2. I eat fruits and vegetables every day.	☐	☐
3. I want to live to be at least 100 years old.	☐	☐
4. I've tried a diet before.	☐	☐
5. I get more exercise now than I did two years ago.	☐	☐
6. To be healthy, I'd rather exercise than eat healthy food.	☐	☐
7. I care about how many calories I eat and drink every day.	☐	☐
8. Even if it's after midnight, I'll eat if I'm hungry.	☐	☐

Listening [1] 07

A Listen to the conversation and decide if the statements are T (true) or F (false).

1. They are eating at a restaurant.   [T / F]
2. The man can't eat bread during his diet.   [T / F]
3. The woman will start a keto diet, too.   [T / F]

B Listen again and answer the comprehension questions.

1. What are three examples of carbs other than vegetables?   _____

2. What are two examples of above-ground vegetables?   _____

3. What food does the woman love?   _____

C Discuss the following questions with your classmates.

1. What kinds of vegetables do you usually eat?
2. Do you think you would be able to be on the keto diet?
3. What would you do if you wanted to lose weight?

Pre-Reading

Think about all of the foods and drinks that you have during a week. Complete the chart. Then, share your answers with your classmates.

	Food / Drink
Often	
Seldom	
Never	

Reading 08

A Read the passage and answer the comprehension questions.

Having a healthy life is important, but what are some of the keys to being healthy? Italy is one of the healthiest countries in the world because of the Mediterranean diet, which includes a large **portion** of vegetables, seafood, extra virgin olive oil, herbs, and bread with a very small amount of red meat. This diet is known to help lower the risk of heart disease, **depression**, cancer, obesity, dementia, Alzheimer's, and Parkinson's diseases. Italians also drink a small amount of red wine, which studies have shown is good for the heart if you drink a glass a day. Many people around the world are on the Mediterranean diet because of the many health **benefits** that it offers.

The traditional foods of Greece, Italy, and Spain are called the Mediterranean diet.

In addition to a good diet, what are other **factors** to being healthy? In looking at countries with healthy diets, health **experts** say that drinking about two liters of water every day and having a lot of plant-based foods such as vegetables, fruits, beans, nuts, and seeds are keys to being healthy. Eating regular-sized portions and having breakfast as your biggest meal of the day are also good for your health.

Breakfast is the most important meal of the day according to health experts.

Having meals with friends and family is also a benefit for good health. This is because people usually eat slower when they are eating with others. It is nice to know that eating while talking with your family or friends is both fun and good for your health. There are many ways to live a healthy life.

....

1. Why is drinking a glass of red wine every day good for you?

   _____

2. What are examples of plant-based foods?

   _____

3. Why is it good to eat with other people?

   _____

B Discuss the following questions with your classmates.

1. What do you usually have for breakfast?
2. What kinds of plant-based food do you usually eat?
3. How long do you usually take to eat each meal?

A Read the conversation and guess the meaning of the idiom.

1. Fill in the blank to complete the idiom. The illustration is a hint.

    A: Did you hear that Emily is becoming a doctor?

    B: Well, it runs in the _____. You know her mother, father, and brother are all doctors.

2. What does the idiom mean?

    a. There is something similar in family members.
    b. There is something different in family members.
    c. There is something unique to only one family member.

B Listen to another conversation and choose the best answer to complete each sentence.

1. The man and the woman are probably _____.

    a. brother and sister　　**b.** teachers　　**c.** students

2. The man doesn't eat or drink any calories for _____.

    a. 24 hours　　**b.** 16 hours　　**c.** 8 hours

3. Many members of the man's family have suffered from _____.

    a. heart disease　　**b.** memory loss　　**c.** skin cancer

4. The fasting diet can improve your _____.

    a. memory　　**b.** hearing　　**c.** eyesight

Writing

Describe your perfect meal. Then, close your textbook and tell your classmates about it.

_____

_____

_____

_____

_____

Food and Health

Technology

Sports

Cultural Differences

Society

Personalization

There are many kinds of diets around the world. Read about three popular diets and answer the questions below. Then, share your answers with your classmates.

	High-Protein Diet	**High-Fiber Diet**	**Low-Calorie Diet**
Benefits	■ strengthens muscles and bones ■ improves metabolism in the body	■ lowers cholesterol levels ■ good for your heart	■ good for quick, short-term weight loss ■ improves mental health
Drawbacks	■ risk of heart disease with too much red meat ■ unsafe for people with kidney problems	■ risk of stomach pain with too much fiber ■ needs more water to balance fiber intake	■ makes you hungry quicker ■ needs careful planning
Recommended	■ meat ■ fish ■ eggs	■ vegetables ■ beans and nuts ■ fruits	■ vegetables ■ fish ■ low-fat or no-fat dairy

1. What is the most important reason you choose the food that you eat?

   _____

2. Which diet do you think would be the best for you?

   _____

3. Which diet do you think would be the most difficult for you?

   _____

4. What other diets do you know about?

   _____

5. If you were cooking a meal, what would you make for each of these diets?
   - High-Protein Diet: _____
   - High-Fiber Diet: _____
   - Low-Calorie Diet: _____

Vocabulary

Read the sentences with the keywords. Then, choose their meanings (a–e) from the box.

1. Smoking, being overweight, and not exercising **contribute** to heart disease. _____

2. One **positive** thing about drinking so much water is that it's good for your skin. _____

3. A **negative** aspect of drinking too much coffee is that you may not sleep well at night. _____

4. I think I will **alter** the recipe by using white sugar instead of brown sugar. _____

5. He was **reluctant** to check his weight after eating so much during the the winter holiday. _____

a. good or useful
b. bad or hurtful
c. change something
d. feeling unsure about doing something
e. add to something to affect someone or something

Warm-Up

A Look at the pictures and answer the questions. Then, share your answers with your classmates.

 playing video games
 smoking
 drinking alcohol
 tanning

1. Why do you think some people enjoy these activities?

   a. _____   b. _____

   c. _____   d. _____

2. What negative health effects can be caused by these activities?

   a. _____   b. _____

   c. _____   d. _____

3. What would you do to reduce the chances of these negative health effects?

   a. _____   b. _____

   c. _____   d. _____

4. Which of these activities do you think is the worst for your health?

   _____

B Put a check (✓) in the box to agree or disagree with each statement below. Then, share your answers with your classmates.

	Agree	Disagree
1. I should see a doctor when I don't feel well.	☐	☐
2. It's important to get a health check once a year.	☐	☐
3. I care more about my health now than I did five years ago.	☐	☐
4. I'm worried about health problems in the future.	☐	☐
5. I'd rather get medicine from a doctor than from a drug store.	☐	☐
6. Doctors in the city are better than doctors in the countryside.	☐	☐
7. I'd rather take medicine for a long time than have surgery.	☐	☐
8. There will be a cure for cancer within the next 10 years.	☐	☐

Listening [1] 11

A Listen to the conversation and decide if the statements are T (true) or F (false).

1. The woman has never donated blood before.   [T / F]
2. The man's blood type is O.   [T / F]
3. The man is afraid of needles.   [T / F]

B Listen again and answer the comprehension questions.

1. Where is the woman going to donate blood?   _____
2. How often does the woman donate blood?   _____
3. What health risks can be lowered by donating blood?   _____

C Discuss the following questions with your classmates.

1. What do you think about when you hear the word "donation"?
2. What do you think about blood donation?
3. Which disease or illness do you think is the scariest?

Pre-Reading

Match the words to the organs (a–e). Then, discuss the following questions with your classmates.

- liver   _____
- brain   _____
- lung(s)   _____
- heart   _____
- kidney(s) _____

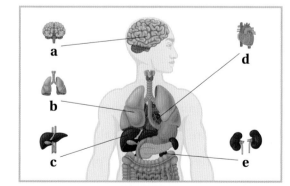

1. What are some things that can damage these organs?
2. Why do you think some people choose to become an organ donor?
3. Why do you think some people choose not to become an organ donor?

Reading

A Read the passage and answer the comprehension questions.

The way you live can **contribute** to your health. Eating food that is high in salt and fat, plus a lack of exercise, can cause a person to become overweight. This can cause high blood pressure which can damage the heart and kidneys. When an organ is in bad condition, an organ donor is needed.

Being overweight can lead to many different health problems.

The choice to become an organ donor is personal. There are **positive** and **negative** aspects to organ donation. Some people become donors because they want to give people a second chance. Some organs, such as a kidney or lung, can be donated while still alive. Other organs, such as the heart, can only be donated after death. It is possible that one donor can save up to 75 people. Some people also donate their body to science. People who do this can help the future of medicine. Doctors and researchers can study these bodies and learn many new things.

People selflessly donate their organs to help others.

Some people choose not to become donors because of religious reasons. For example, one religion believes that a person's spirit is linked to the body and only God can **alter** it. There is another reason some people are **reluctant** to donate: They don't want to help people who haven't taken care of their health. They believe that a person shouldn't get a new liver, for instance, if the disease is due to drinking too much alcohol. While each person and situation are different, there are many things to think about before agreeing to become an organ donor.

1. Why is high blood pressure bad?

   _____

2. How many people can be saved by one organ donor?

   _____

3. What is the reason some people think others don't deserve organ donation?

   _____

B Discuss the following questions with your classmates.

1. What can you do to lower high blood pressure?

2. Would you rather donate organs while still alive or donate them after death?

3. Do you agree or disagree that some people don't deserve organ donation?

Listening [2] 13

A Read the conversation and guess the meaning of the idiom.

1. Fill in the blank to complete the idiom. The illustration is a hint.

    A: I agree with you that ice cream can be eaten at any time!

    B: I'm glad we're on the same _____ about that. My family always says I'm crazy for eating ice cream at midnight.

2. What does the idiom mean?

    a. People have many opinions.

    b. People have unpopular opinions.

    c. People have the same opinion.

B Listen to another conversation and choose the best answer to complete each sentence.

1. The man and the woman are probably _____.

    a. husband and wife   **b.** doctor and nurse   **c.** brother and sister

2. The transplant will happen _____.

    a. months later   **b.** years from now   **c.** soon

3. The man is not able to donate because of his _____.

    a. religious beliefs   **b.** blood type   **c.** kidney disease

4. A transplanted kidney from a living donor lasts _____ as long as one from a non-living donor.

    a. twice   **b.** just   **c.** half

Writing

Describe some healthy and unhealthy things you do. Then, close your textbook and tell your classmates about it.

_____

_____

_____

_____

_____

Personalization

There are many factors to staying healthy. Answer the questions below and calculate your points. Then, share your result with your classmates.

1. How often do you have breakfast in the morning?

   a. every day   **b.** almost every day   **c.** sometimes

   d. hardly ever   **e.** never

2. How often do you exercise?

   a. every day   **b.** almost every day   **c.** sometimes

   d. hardly ever   **e.** never

3. How often do you eat sweets?

   a. every day   **b.** almost every day   **c.** sometimes

   d. hardly ever   **e.** never

4. How often do you eat snacks between meals?

   a. never   **b.** hardly ever   **c.** sometimes

   d. almost every day   **e.** every day

5. How often do you eat after 10:00 p.m.?

   a. never   **b.** hardly ever   **c.** sometimes

   d. almost every day   **e.** every day

6. How long do you usually sleep at night?

   a. more than 8 hours   **b.** about 6–8 hours   **c.** about 5–7 hours

   d. about 3–5 hours   **e.** less than 3 hours

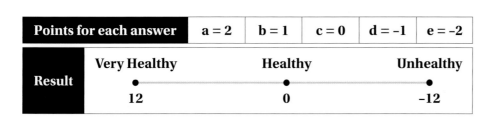

Points for each answer	a = 2	b = 1	c = 0	d = –1	e = –2

Result	Very Healthy	Healthy	Unhealthy
	12	0	–12

Your points	a	b	c	d	e	Total	

Your result	

Wrap-Up

Answer the questions. Then, share your answers with your classmates.

Unit 1   Food and Culture

1. What are some foods that have recently become popular in your country?

2. Which areas in your country are popular for their food?

3. What are some foods that you and your family eat on special occasions?

Unit 2   Diets

4. What do you think is the best reason to start a diet?

5. What would be the biggest factor in ending a diet?

6. What do you think is the best way to stay healthy?

Unit 3   Saving Lives

7. When you are not feeling well, what kinds of foods and drinks do you usually have?

8. If you had a health problem, who would you talk with first?

9. What do you think about transplanting animal organs to humans?

Technology

Improvements in technology continue to make our lives more convenient.
With this technology, however, there are dangers and risks.

Unit 4 Identity Theft

"Your date of birth is a security point for identity theft."
Adam Conover

Unit 5 Digital Learning

"Technology is just a tool. In terms of getting the kids working together and motivating them, the teacher is the most important."
Bill Gates

Unit 6 Artificial Intelligence

"AI will probably most likely lead to the end of the world, but in the meantime, there'll be great companies."
Sam Altman

Unit 4   Identity Theft

Vocabulary

Read the sentences with the keywords. Then, choose their meanings (a–e) from the box.

1. From time to time, you still need to renew your **license** to be a doctor. _____

2. The biggest **impact** of losing my phone is that I couldn't communicate with my friends. _____

3. Thieves **target** tourists, so it's important to be careful when you are overseas. _____

4. You need a fingerprint and a key to enter, so the **security** for this building is good. _____

5. Because I could **acquire** a new microphone, my online videos sound much better now. _____

> **a.** a big effect
> **b.** get something
> **c.** a system that has been created to make you feel safe
> **d.** an official document or card that lets you do something
> **e.** try to attack or act against someone or something

Warm-Up

A Look at the pictures and answer the questions. Then, share your answers with your classmates.

a. shop online

b. use your phone in public

c. write down your password

d. lose your wallet

1. How often do you do these things?

   a. _____   b. _____

   c. _____   d. _____

2. What risks could result from doing these things?

   a. _____   b. _____

   c. _____   d. _____

3. How can you lower the possibility of such risks?

   a. _____   b. _____

   c. _____   d. _____

4. Have you ever had anything stolen before? If yes, what was it?

   _____

B Put a check (✓) in the box to agree or disagree with each statement below. Then, share your answers with your classmates.

	Agree	Disagree
1. I always feel safe in my hometown.	☐	☐
2. I'd rather lose my wallet than my phone.	☐	☐
3. I think the information on my computer is safe.	☐	☐
4. I feel that social networking sites are safe.	☐	☐
5. I never share personal data online.	☐	☐
6. My passwords are simple and easy to remember.	☐	☐
7. I'm worried about online security.	☐	☐
8. There will be more cyberattacks in the future.	☐	☐

Unit 1
Unit 2
Unit 3
Unit 4
Unit 5
Unit 6
Unit 7
Unit 8
Unit 9
Unit 10
Unit 11
Unit 12
Unit 13
Unit 14
Unit 15

Listening [1] 15

A Listen to the conversation and decide if the statements are T (true) or F (false).

1. The man thinks his wallet was stolen on the train.   [T / F]
2. The woman has had her purse stolen before.   [T / F]
3. The woman is the manager of the man's apartment.   [T / F]

B Listen again and answer the comprehension questions.

1. Where does the man usually keep his wallet?   _____

2. Why does the man still have his train pass?   _____

3. What was in the wallet except credit cards and money?   _____

C Discuss the following questions with your classmates.

1. Where do you usually keep your wallet?
2. What would you do if you found someone's wallet?
3. What kinds of things have you ever lost?

Pre-Reading

What could happen if someone steals the items below? Complete the chart. Then, share your answers with your classmates.

	Item	What could happen?
1	smartphone	
2	credit card	
3	passport	
4	driver's license	

Reading 16

A Read the passage and answer the comprehension questions.

Identity theft is a crime where one person takes someone's personal information. This information can then be used to make new bank accounts, credit cards, and driver's **licenses**. Here is an example of how identity theft can hurt someone: A thief uses someone else's identity, gets a speeding ticket, and doesn't pay for it. Although a speeding ticket for driving too fast seems like a small thing, the victim can be arrested by the police without knowing what is happening.

There are many different ways to take someone's things.

Even before the growth in technology, identity theft happened and many people had their wallets or valuables stolen. However, the loss was usually small. Now, the **impact** is much bigger. Since so much personal data is saved in computers, identity thieves or cyber hackers **target** people and companies online in order to get personal information.

Cyber hackers steal personal data online.

Thieves can get such information from public computers and public Wi-Fi where **security** is not strong. Once thieves **acquire** the personal information, they are able to log in to emails, shopping sites, and everything else that has been used by the victims. In 2020, 49 million Americans became victims of identity theft and lost 56 billion dollars in total. In addition to the financial loss, some victims have emotional stress as well. While technology has made things like shopping much more convenient, it has also made it easier for people to have their identity stolen.

∙∙

1. What are three things that can be made with someone's personal information?

_____

2. Who do identity thieves or cyber hackers target?

_____

3. Where can thieves get personal information from?

_____

B Discuss the following questions with your classmates.

1. Who would you call first if you were in trouble?

2. Have you ever received a call from a stranger? If yes, how did you feel at that time?

3. In what situation do you use public Wi-Fi the most?

Unit 1
Unit 2
Unit 3
Unit 4
Unit 5
Unit 6
Unit 7
Unit 8
Unit 9
Unit 10
Unit 11
Unit 12
Unit 13
Unit 14
Unit 15

Listening [2] 🎧

A Read the conversation and guess the meaning of the idiom.

1. Fill in the blank to complete the idiom. The illustration is a hint.

    A: I forgot my driver's license. I've got to drive home to pick it up.

    B: Well, why play with _____? What will you do
    if the police catch you? I'll drive you home.

2. What does the idiom mean?

    a. Someone does something fun.

    b. Someone does something new.

    c. Someone does something risky.

B Listen to another conversation and choose the best answer to complete each sentence.

1. The man and the woman are probably _____.

    a. cyber hackers   **b.** students   **c.** co-workers

2. The woman says that VPNs _____.

    a. come with different prices   **b.** are free   **c.** have problems

3. The man has _____ at this café before.

    a. not used Wi-Fi   **b.** used a free VPN   **c.** not had a problem

4. The woman says that the man would be in trouble because he is _____.

    a. buying a cheap VPN   **b.** coming to this café   **c.** not using a VPN

Writing

Describe a time you lost something important to you. Then, close your textbook and tell your
classmates about it.

_____

_____

_____

_____

_____

Personalization

There are weak and strong passwords. Look at the examples and answer the questions below. Then, calculate your points and share your result with your classmates.

Example	Weak Password	Strong Password
	emiko	em1k0
	emiko0210	em1k0Febtenth
	password	Pa$sw0rd
	emiko	emeekkoh

Question	Points	
	Yes	No
1. Are your passwords more than seven characters?	+1	0
2. Are your passwords more than nine characters?	+5	0
3. Do you use both lower- and upper-case letters in your passwords?	+1	0
4. Do you have numbers in your passwords?	+2	0
5. Do you have special characters like !, &, ?, %, and # in your passwords?	+3	0
6. Do you only have a number or special character at the end of your passwords?	–1	0
7. Do you ever change your passwords?	+1	0
8. Do you change your important passwords at least once a year?	+3	0
9. Do you have keyboard sequences like "qwerty" or "asdfgh" in your passwords?	–5	0
10. Do your passwords include some words like "password," "pw," or "pass"?	–20	0
11. Do you use a letter or number in your passwords more than twice like "aaa" or "222"?	–10	0
12. Do your passwords include any part of your name or your birthday?	–15	0
13. Do you use the same password on many different websites?	–50	0
14. Have you ever shared your passwords with someone else?	–10	0
15. Do you keep your passwords in an email, unprotected file, or on a piece of paper?	–20	0

Total

Total	Result
Less than –50	It's dangerous. Change your passwords right now!
–50 to 0	Your passwords are easy for people to guess. You'd better change them now.
1 to 15	Your passwords are pretty good. You are probably safe.
More than 15	Wonderful! You can relax because your passwords are strong.

Unit 5 Digital Learning

Vocabulary 18

Read the sentences with the keywords. Then, choose their meanings (a–e) from the box.

1. Recently, more classes have started to **incorporate** videos and online tasks. _____

2. Technology is **defined** as the use of scientific knowledge in different ways. _____

3. I bought a new **device** that sends me a text when homework is due. _____

4. I need to remember to **submit** my project before I leave for summer vacation. _____

5. I can't **focus** on studying in the library because it's too quiet. _____

a. explain the meaning of something
b. give your attention to something
c. an object that is used for a special purpose
d. give a document or something to someone to be looked at
e. use something as part of a bigger thing

Warm-Up

A Look at the pictures and answer the questions. Then, share your answers with your classmates.

kindergarten

elementary school

junior high school

high school

1. In your country, at what ages do you start going to these schools?

    a. _____   b. _____

    c. _____   d. _____

2. What did you enjoy at each of these schools the most?

    a. _____   b. _____

    c. _____   d. _____

3. What are some skills you learned at each of these schools?

    a. _____   b. _____

    c. _____   d. _____

4. If you could go back to any grade, which grade would you choose?

    _____

B Put a check (✓) in the box to agree or disagree with each statement below. Then, share your answers with your classmates.

	Agree	Disagree
1. I enjoy being a student.	☐	☐
2. I can type quickly.	☐	☐
3. I can find information quickly on the Internet.	☐	☐
4. I enjoy online lessons.	☐	☐
5. Comic books are better in print than on a digital device.	☐	☐
6. It's important to learn computer skills for my future job.	☐	☐
7. At restaurants, I prefer to order from a tablet than a printed menu.	☐	☐
8. Within the next 20 years, there will be no printed newspapers.	☐	☐

Listening [1] 🎧 19

A Listen to the conversation and decide if the statements are T (true) or F (false).

1. The man's school will start using tablets soon.   [T / F]
2. The woman says she types quickly.   [T / F]
3. The woman says she is very organized.   [T / F]

B Listen again and answer the comprehension questions.

1. How does the woman feel about using a tablet at school? _____

2. What are two reasons why the man prefers books? _____

3. What are three things the woman has on her tablet? _____

C Discuss the following questions with your classmates.

1. How would you feel if your school switched from textbooks to tablets?

2. In which situations are digital books better than physical books?

3. What are the negative points of using a tablet to study?

Pre-Reading

How do you feel about technology in the classroom? Complete the chart. Then, share your answers with your classmates.

	I would rather ...		Reason
1	do research	☐ in a library. ☐ on the Internet at home.	
2	learn from	☐ a whiteboard or chalkboard. ☐ a slideshow.	
3	take notes with	☐ a pen or pencil. ☐ a digital pen or stylus.	

Reading 🎧 20

A Read the passage and answer the comprehension questions.

We live in a digital age where technology is around us every day. As a result, more and more schools are starting to **incorporate** digital learning into their classrooms. Digital learning can be **defined** as learning that uses technology. There are many ways in which digital learning can be used, so it is important to think about the benefits and drawbacks of digital learning in classrooms.

Digital learning can give students less to carry when they go to school.

The use of digital **devices** instead of textbooks is a part of digital learning. Students can have their textbooks on a tablet or computer instead of carrying many books in a bag. This is convenient for students, especially if they have a long commute to school. Also, students who use digital learning can complete a variety of tasks on the devices, such as creating digital presentations, editing videos, and **submitting** assignments online. These activities help students learn skills that can be useful for their future careers.

Some students may lose conversation skills when they use digital devices too often.

One of the negative aspects of digital learning is looking at a screen for a long time. It can damage the eyesight of students. Additionally, students may use their devices to access games and social media accounts rather than lesson information. Also, some experts say that students lose conversation skills in digital classrooms because they tend to **focus** more on the screen in front of them than the person next to them. As technology develops, schools will be required to look for better ways to use digital learning in their classrooms.

....

1. How is digital learning defined?

_____

2. What are three tasks that students can do on digital devices?

_____

3. What is the reason some experts say students can lose conversational skills in a digital classroom?

_____

B Discuss the following questions with your classmates.

1. What learning tasks have you done with your tablet or computer?

2. Which of these tasks do you think was the most useful?

3. Do you agree or disagree that students can lose conversational skills in a digital classroom?

Unit 1 Unit 2 Unit 3 Unit 4 Unit 5 Unit 6 Unit 7 Unit 8 Unit 9 Unit 10 Unit 11 Unit 12 Unit 13 Unit 14 Unit 15

Listening [2] 21

A   Read the conversation and guess the meaning of the idiom.

1. Fill in the blank to complete the idiom. The illustration is a hint.

   A: Do you know Jason Thompson?

   B: That name rings a _____. We may have
   had a class together before.

2. What does the idiom mean?

   a. Someone or something is clearly remembered.

   b. Someone or something is barely remembered.

   c. Someone or something is forgotten.

B   Listen to another conversation and choose the best answer to complete each sentence.

1. The man and the woman are probably _____ school.

   a. teachers at the same   **b.** students at the same   **c.** students at an online

2. The woman is taking a French class at _____.

   a. a school in Belgium   **b.** a school in France   **c.** her school online

3. The man doesn't remember the announcement because _____ email.

   a. there was no   **b.** he didn't read the   **c.** he didn't understand the

4. According to the woman, there are _____ students from Asia and Europe in her new class.

   a. 13   **b.** 15   **c.** 30

Writing

Describe some positives and negatives of taking online classes. Then, close your textbook and
tell your classmates about it.

_____

_____

_____

_____

_____

Personalization

There are many reasons for wanting to take online or face-to-face classes. Complete the information below. Then, share your answers with your classmates.

1. If I had a class early in the morning, I'd rather take [an online / a face-to-face] class because _____
   _____
   _____ .

2. If it took me more than 20 minutes to get to school, I'd rather take [an online / a face-to-face] class because _____
   _____
   _____ .

3. If I had a class with more than 50 students in it, I'd rather take [an online / a face-to-face] class because _____
   _____
   _____ .

4. If I had a discussion-based class, I'd rather take [an online / a face-to-face] class because _____
   _____
   _____ .

5. If I had a pet to take care of, I'd rather take [an online / a face-to-face] class because _____
   _____
   _____ .

6. If I had an exam, I'd rather take [an online / a face-to-face] class because _____
   _____
   _____ .

Unit **6**   Artificial Intelligence

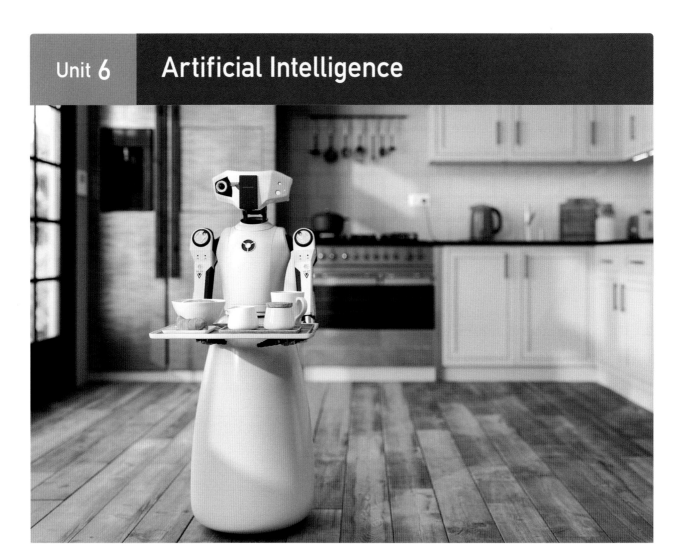

Vocabulary

Read the sentences with the keywords. Then, choose their meanings (a–e) from the box.

1. I prefer to **purchase** my clothes from a shop rather than online.   ____

2. This phone application can **assist** your diet by showing how many calories are in your food.   ____

3. It's **obvious** that technology has made our lives more convenient.   ____

4. I can't imagine a **scenario** where cars will be flying.   ____

5. A camera will **monitor** the students during the test to make sure no one is cheating.   ____

---

a. a situation of something that could happen

b. watch someone or something for a special reason

c. easy to see or know about

d. buy something

e. help someone or something

Warm-Up

A Look at the pictures and answer the questions. Then, share your answers with your classmates.

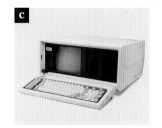

1. These are old versions of electronic items. What are they?

   a. _____   b. _____

   c. _____   d. _____

2. What is the biggest difference between these old versions and the newest versions?

   a. _____   b. _____

   c. _____   d. _____

3. How often do you use these items?

   a. _____   b. _____

   c. _____   d. _____

4. What new electronic item would you like to see made in the future?

   _____

B Put a check (✓) in the box to agree or disagree with each statement below. Then, share your answers with your classmates.

		Agree	Disagree
1.	Technology makes us lazy.	☐	☐
2.	We don't need more technology in our lives.	☐	☐
3.	I understand how AI is used.	☐	☐
4.	I use AI almost every day.	☐	☐
5.	Most AI that I know about comes from movies and television programs.	☐	☐
6.	When I think of AI, I think of robots.	☐	☐
7.	In the future, robots will take jobs away from people.	☐	☐
8.	In the future, AI will be smarter than people.	☐	☐

Listening [1] 23

A Listen to the conversation and decide if the statements are T (true) or F (false).

1. The man went to bed at 9:00 p.m.   [T / F]
2. The woman shops online.   [T / F]
3. The woman also missed the quiz.   [T / F]

B Listen again and answer the comprehension questions.

1. What kind of movie did the man watch?
2. Why does the woman have so many part-time jobs?
3. When will the man take the quiz?

C Discuss the following questions with your classmates.

1. How much time do you usually spend watching streaming services?
2. Which do you prefer, watching movies at home or going to a movie theater?
3. Do you think the AI recommendations on websites are useful or dangerous?

Pre-Reading

Do you know about these AI items? Complete the chart. Then, share your answers with your classmates.

	Name	Function	Where is it used?
1	Pepper		
2	Roomba		
3	Echo		

Reading 🎧24

A Read the passage and answer the comprehension questions.

The use of artificial intelligence (AI) is everywhere. Millions of people around the world use Siri, Google Now, and Cortana on their smartphones. If you **purchase** something on a shopping site like eBay or Amazon, the company may use AI to track your purchase history and recommend products they think you may like. The improvements in AI have also made video games more enjoyable for people around the world.

Websites like eBay use artificial intelligence to recommend things you may like.

Besides entertainment, AI can be very helpful in society. Recently, hotels and restaurants have begun to use robots and machines with AI as their staff. Using robots instead of people can save workers from working in the early morning or late at night. Also, AI doesn't make mistakes and never gets tired or feels stress.

While AI can **assist** and entertain us, there are dangers as well. The most **obvious** danger is military use around the world. They can use AI in battlefield robots and drones. Since the machines are programmed

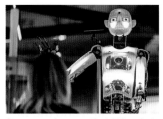
Some people worry that AI in robots could make them too intelligent.

by humans, there is a risk. Stephen Hawking once said that he fears AI battlefield robots will be much smarter in the future, so they will be able to make decisions on their own to kill someone. While his **scenario** doesn't suggest a situation like *Terminator* where robots attack the world, a robot killing even one person is not acceptable. Although we enjoy the benefits of AI in our lives, it is important to **monitor** it closely in the future.

1. What are three examples of AI on smartphones?

2. Where are two places that AI has been used as staff in place of people?

3. What are two examples of the use of AI in militaries around the world?

B Discuss the following questions with your classmates.

1. How often do you use an AI assistant on your smartphone?
2. What do you think about working with an AI robot or machine at your job?
3. Should robots and machines be developed to make decisions by themselves?

Listening [2]

A Read the conversation and guess the meaning of the idiom.

1. Fill in the blank to complete the idiom. The illustration is a hint.

   A: I've heard today's test has been postponed. We have to prepare for it again!

   B: Well, let's see the glass as half full, not half _____.
   We have more time to study now.

2. What does the idiom mean?

   a. Let's see things in the past, not in the future.
   b. Let's see things in a positive way, not in a negative way.
   c. Let's see things in an old way, not in a new way.

B Listen to another conversation and choose the best answer to complete each sentence.

1. The man and the woman are probably _____.

   a. at a car dealer   **b.** in a factory   **c.** in a mall

2. The woman believes that _____ are good for customers.

   a. robots   **b.** self-checkout registers   **c.** aging workers

3. The man believes machines _____.

   a. take jobs away from people   **b.** make jobs easier   **c.** make more jobs for people

4. The woman says that robots and AI will _____.

   a. become managers   **b.** help humans   **c.** also age

Writing

Describe some positives and negatives of using even better AI in the future. Then, close your textbook and tell your classmates about it.

_____

_____

_____

_____

_____

Personalization

The development of AI will change many things in the future. Decide the chance of this happening for the following situations from 1 (less likely) to 5 (most likely). Then, share your answers with your classmates.

Situation in the Future		Chance of It Happening
1. 	Virtual reality (VR) will be so good that people will not want to travel.	[1 / 2 / 3 / 4 / 5]
2. 	Artificial pets will become more popular than real pets.	[1 / 2 / 3 / 4 / 5]
3. 	It will be difficult to tell who is human and who is a robot.	[1 / 2 / 3 / 4 / 5]
4. 	All cars will move without drivers.	[1 / 2 / 3 / 4 / 5]
5. 	Washing machines will do the laundry, dry clothes, and fold them.	[1 / 2 / 3 / 4 / 5]
6. 	Marriage between a robot and a human will happen.	[1 / 2 / 3 / 4 / 5]
7. 	Drones will be used in a more negative and dangerous way.	[1 / 2 / 3 / 4 / 5]

Wrap-Up

Answer the questions. Then, share your answers with your classmates.

Unit 4 Identity Theft

1. What are some things you do to help remember your passwords?

2. Which do you think is worse, physical theft or online theft?

3. What would worry you the most if your identity was stolen?

Unit 5 Digital Learning

4. What do you think are the biggest benefits of digital learning?

5. How is technology used at your school or workplace?

6. What do you think about studying abroad online?

Unit 6 Artificial Intelligence

7. How can AI help people over the age of 70?

8. Where do you think more AI should be used?

9. What are the biggest advantages and disadvantages of AI?

Sports

Billions of people around the world watch sports every year.
World-class athletes receive multi-million-dollar salaries due to their years of time and training.

Unit 7 Professional Athletes

"I'm not paid to be a role model, parents should be role models."
Charles Barkley

Unit 8 The Olympics

"Just going to the Olympics would be a dream come true. I could finish last, and it would still be an amazing experience."
Chloe Kim

Unit 9 Cheating

"I would prefer even to fail with honor than win by cheating."
Sophocles

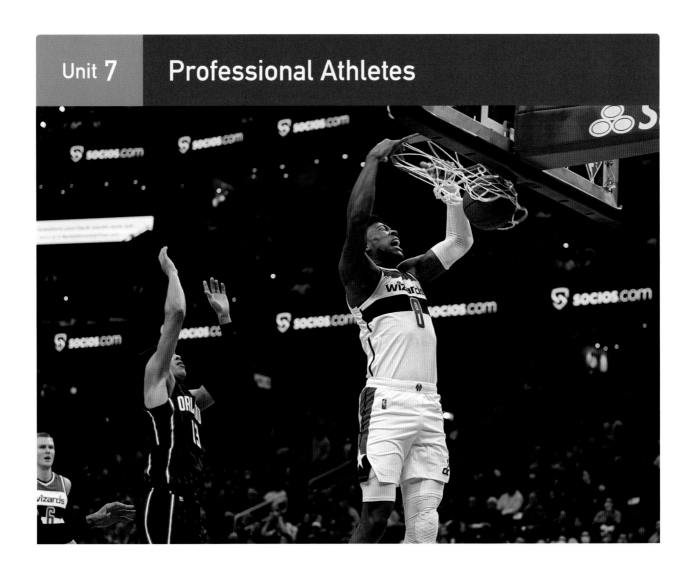

Vocabulary

Read the sentences with the keywords. Then, choose their meanings (a–e) from the box.

1. I wanted to become a **professional** tennis player to be rich and famous.   _____

2. Many countries are **involved** in the Olympics and the World Cup.   _____

3. There is a **debate** about what is the most popular sport in the world.   _____

4. There is a **finite** number of people who can become professional athletes.   _____

5. Using sponsor names for the naming of stadiums has become an **issue** for some fans.   _____

> a. include someone as part of something
> b. a topic of discussion
> c. having a limit
> d. getting paid for something as a job instead of a hobby
> e. a discussion where people give different opinions

Warm-Up

A Look at the pictures and answer the questions. Then, share your answers with your classmates.

1. What countries are famous for the sport in each picture?

   a. _____   b. _____

   c. _____   d. _____

2. Who are some athletes that play these sports?

   a. _____   b. _____

   c. _____   d. _____

3. How often do you watch these sports?

   a. _____   b. _____

   c. _____   d. _____

4. What sport do you think is the most popular in your country?

   _____

B Put a check (✓) in the box to agree or disagree with each statement below. Then, share your answers with your classmates.

	Agree	Disagree
1. I'm good at sports.	☐	☐
2. I've been to a professional sporting event.	☐	☐
3. I prefer watching sports to playing sports.	☐	☐
4. Team sports are better than individual sports.	☐	☐
5. Sports fans are too emotional about sports.	☐	☐
6. I'd like to meet a professional athlete.	☐	☐
7. If I had the ability, I'd like to be a professional athlete.	☐	☐
8. The salaries of professional athletes are too high.	☐	☐

Listening [1] 27

A Listen to the conversation and decide if the statements are T (true) or F (false).

1. They are waiting for the game to start. [T / F]
2. The man used to be good at sports. [T / F]
3. The man is a scientist. [T / F]

B Listen again and answer the comprehension questions.

1. Where are they now? _____

2. What did the woman want to be when she was younger? _____

3. What was the reason for the man to give up his dream? _____

C Discuss the following questions with your classmates.

1. What do you think about sports?

2. Is it better to watch sports in a stadium or on TV?

3. What did you want to be when you were younger?

Pre-Reading

Should professional athletes earn the highest salary among other jobs? Rank the jobs according to ideal salaries from 1 (highest) to 8 (lowest). Then, share your answers with your classmates.

architect

athlete

doctor

movie star

pilot

police officer

scientist

teacher

Reading 🎧 28

A Read the passage and answer the comprehension questions.

Millions of children dream of being **professional** athletes and becoming rich and famous. The average salary for great athletes around the world is about 20 million dollars a year and the very best can make over 100 million dollars with their salary plus money from company advertising. One reason for this huge amount of money is that superstar athletes help make their teams rich. For example, Real Madrid and Barcelona are both worth about 5 billion dollars.

Real Madrid is one of the most valuable teams in the world.

With the money **involved** in professional sports, there is a **debate** about the salaries. The average doctor's salary in the US is a little over 300 thousand dollars and a teacher makes only about 60 thousand dollars a year. Some believe that because athletes' careers are **finite**, it is OK to make millions of dollars. Others think that athletes shouldn't get paid that much for just playing games and it is unfair compared to doctors saving lives and teachers educating children.

Tiger Woods used to be a role model for many children.

Another **issue** is whether athletes are role models. Retired professional basketball player, Charles Barkley once famously said, "I am not a role model." His argument was that children should look to their parents or people they know as role models, not athletes. Tiger Woods was once a role model for many children until his scandals. However, some people now praise how he has come through difficult times. The truth is, we only know superstar athletes from what we see on television or the Internet.

∙∙

1. Why do some people believe athletes should get a high salary?

   _____

2. Why do some people think athletes shouldn't get a high salary?

   _____

3. Why do some people now praise Tiger Woods?

   _____

B Discuss the following questions with your classmates.

1. What do you think about professional athletes' salaries?

2. Whom do you think children should look to as role models?

3. Who is your role model?

Listening [2] 29

A Read the conversation and guess the meaning of the idiom.

1. Fill in the blank to complete the idiom. The illustration is a hint.

   A: Can you buy me lunch?

   B: What? Don't you know that money doesn't _____ on trees?

   A: I know, but I forgot my wallet again.

2. What does the idiom mean?

   a. It is good to borrow money from someone.

   b. It is easy to lose money.

   c. It isn't easy to earn money.

B Listen to another conversation and choose the best answer to complete each sentence.

1. The woman is probably talking with _____.

   a. her brother   **b.** her co-worker   **c.** her student

2. The man and the woman think professional athletes should get paid _____ money.

   a. less   **b.** a little more   **c.** a lot more

3. The woman thinks that many people want to be _____.

   a. fashion models   **b.** professional athletes   **c.** rich

4. The man thinks that some professional athletes don't _____.

   a. use their money well   **b.** like money   **c.** grow trees

Writing

Describe what you would do if you had a lot of money. Then, close your textbook and tell your classmates about it.

_____

_____

_____

_____

_____

Personalization

Many professional athletes spend a huge amount of money on a variety of things. Decide if the examples below are worthwhile or not and write reasons. Then, share your answers with your classmates.

Example	Worthwhile or not?
1.  Buying many expensive cars	
2.  Owning sharks in a private aquarium	
3.  Building schools in a developing country	
4.  Traveling by a private jet	
5. Purchasing a luxurious mansion	
6. Having a movie theater at home	
7.  Donating money to charities	

Unit 8 **The Olympics**

Vocabulary

Read the sentences with the keywords. Then, choose their meanings (a–e) from the box.

1. The **financial** cost of hosting the Olympics is huge. _____

2. His **primary** goal of becoming an athlete is to be a gold medal winner for his country. _____

3. **Infrastructure**, such as the Shinkansen, developed due to the 1964 Olympics. _____

4. The new sports **facility** will have a climbing wall and an indoor running track. _____

5. Because they didn't **maintain** the stadium very well, they will need to build a new one soon. _____

a. a building or place that is used for different activities
b. keep something in good condition
c. having to do with money
d. main or most important
e. a basic system for a society such as transportation or power supplies

56

Warm-Up

A Look at the pictures and answer the questions. Then, share your answers with your classmates.

1. What is the name of the sport in each picture?

    a. _____ b. _____

    c. _____ d. _____

2. What kind of facilities are the sports played in?

    a. _____ b. _____

    c. _____ d. _____

3. What is some equipment needed for each sport?

    a. _____ b. _____

    c. _____ d. _____

4. Which do you prefer, the Summer Olympics or the Winter Olympics?

    _____

B Put a check (✓) in the box to agree or disagree with each statement below. Then, share your answers with your classmates.

		Agree	Disagree
1.	I'm interested in the Olympics.	☐	☐
2.	I'd like to go and watch the Olympics.	☐	☐
3.	I think it would be wonderful to win a gold medal.	☐	☐
4.	When I watch the Olympics, I feel like playing sports.	☐	☐
5.	I'm proud of my country when I watch the Olympics.	☐	☐
6.	I'd like my country to host the Olympics.	☐	☐
7.	The Olympics are a good chance to learn about other countries and cultures.	☐	☐
8.	I think that a lot of athletes take drugs to try to win an Olympic medal.	☐	☐

Listening [1]

A Listen to the conversation and decide if the statements are T (true) or F (false).

1. The man has attended the Summer Olympics. [T / F]
2. The woman likes watching the opening ceremony. [T / F]
3. They think winning an Olympic medal is important. [T / F]

B Listen again and answer the comprehension questions.

1. What winter sport does the man like? _____

2. What winter sports does the woman like? _____

3. What does the man like about the Olympics? _____

C Discuss the following questions with your classmates.

1. Which sports do you enjoy playing?

2. If your country hosted the Olympics, what performances and clothing would be in the ceremonies?

3. What do you think are some examples of good sportsmanship?

Pre-Reading

How much do you know about the Olympics? Answer the questions. Then, share your answers with your classmates.

	Question	Answer
1	How much silver and pure gold are required to be in a gold medal?	
2	The Olympics were canceled in 1916, 1940, and 1944. What were the reasons?	
3	What do the five colors of the Olympic rings mean?	
4	What information above is the most surprising to you?	

Reading

A Read the passage and answer the comprehension questions.

Many people around the world have been wondering if hosting the Olympics is worth its **financial** cost. Beijing spent over 40 billion dollars for the 2008 Summer Olympics and Sochi spent over 50 billion dollars for the 2014 Winter Olympics. The **primary** costs of hosting the Olympics are for security and **infrastructure**. Also, remodeling of hotels, highways, transportation systems, and sports **facilities** is necessary.

The Bird's Nest Stadium in Beijing cost over 400 million dollars to build.

Many cities and countries have spent the money to introduce themselves to the world. Berlin in 1936 was the first city to use the Olympics as a global showcase which was broadcast on television. Cities such as Tokyo in 1964 and Munich in 1972 hosted the Olympics to show the world how their countries had changed since World War II. Barcelona became an international destination for many travelers after the 1992 Summer Olympics.

The lighting of the Olympic flame in Montreal.

Not all host cities benefit from the Olympics, however. High cost is one reason. Montreal hosted the 1976 Summer Olympics and took nearly 30 years to pay back the money it spent. Athens hosted the Olympics in 2004 and built many expensive stadiums and sports facilities. After the Olympics, they didn't have enough money to **maintain** the facilities, and many were never used again. Unfortunately, high costs are not the only problem that can happen during the Olympics. Munich and Atlanta are more memorable for terrorist acts than for the athletic performances. Host cities must decide if the benefits of hosting the Olympics are worth the risks.

1. What are two main reasons the Olympics is so expensive?

2. What happened to Barcelona after the 1992 Olympics?

3. What happened at the Munich and Atlanta Olympics?

B Discuss the following questions with your classmates.

1. Which should be used for the Olympics; a new stadium, a remodeled stadium, or an old stadium?
2. Do you think your country would benefit from hosting the Olympics?
3. What are other things a country could spend billions of dollars on instead of the Olympics?

Listening [2] 33

A Read the conversation and guess the meaning of the idiom.

1. Fill in the blanks to complete the idiom. The illustration is a hint.

   A: I bought diamond earrings for my girlfriend.

   B: They must have cost an _____ and a _____!

   A: They sure did. I need to find another part-time job.

2. What does the idiom mean?

   a. They are very expensive.

   b. They are gorgeous.

   c. They are memorable.

B Listen to another conversation and choose the best answer to complete each sentence.

1. The man is probably talking with his _____.

   a. friend   **b.** sister   **c.** wife

2. The man and the woman are _____ about their city hosting the Olympics.

   a. excited   **b.** unhappy   **c.** surprised

3. For the woman, the best thing about the Olympics is _____.

   a. the people   **b.** the new facilities   **c.** a better subway system

4. The man will probably _____ during the Olympics.

   a. watch TV at home   **b.** be out of the city   **c.** stay at a hotel

Writing

Describe how you would feel if your country became the host of the next Olympics. Then, close your textbook and tell your classmates about it.

_____

_____

_____

_____

_____

Personalization

There are many different views on the Olympics. Decide if the situations below are benefits or drawbacks and write reasons. Then, share your answers with your classmates.

Situation	Benefit / Drawback
 1. It is expensive for a city to host the Olympics.	
 2. A host city is at risk for terrorist activities.	
 3. Many companies advertise their products at the Olympics.	
 4. Many people volunteer for the Olympics.	
5. Citizens in the host city are inconvenienced during the Olympics.	
 6. More tourists visit the host city after the Olympics.	
 7. The host city becomes more multicultural after the Olympics.	

Unit 9   Cheating

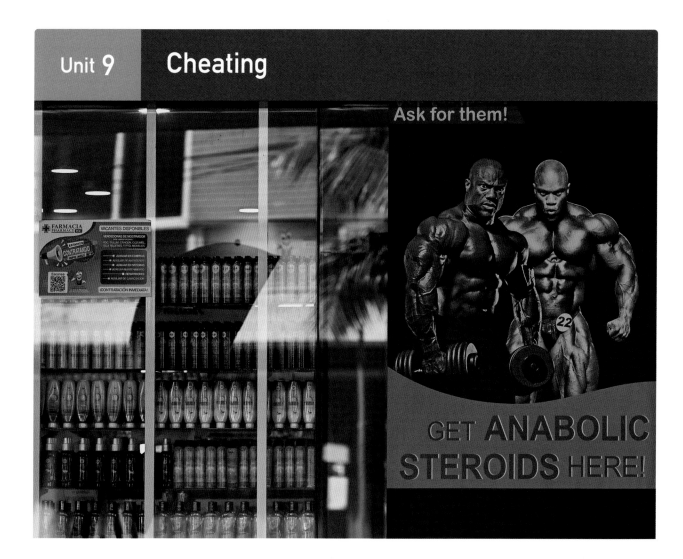

Vocabulary

Read the sentences with the keywords. Then, choose their meanings (a–e) from the box.

1. There is an **inclination** to eat protein so you can gain muscle. _____

2. Drug tests **expose** which athletes cheat. _____

3. He **schemed** to win the game by secretly watching the other team practice. _____

4. It's **illegal** to become a better athlete by using drugs. _____

5. I'm trying to **enhance** my performance without breaking the rules. _____

> a. not allowed by law
> b. make something better
> c. a feeling making you want to do something
> d. make something negative public
> e. plan to do something that is not honest

Warm-Up

A Look at the pictures and answer the questions. Then, share your answers with your classmates.

1. What are some reasons that athletes decide to cheat?

   a. _____   b. _____

   c. _____   d. _____

2. Which sports do you think professional athletes have cheated in for these reasons?

   a. _____   b. _____

   c. _____   d. _____

3. How do you think professional athletes have cheated because of these reasons?

   a. _____   b. _____

   c. _____   d. _____

4. If no one knows you have cheated, is it still cheating?

   _____

B Put a check (✓) in the box to agree or disagree with each statement below. Then, share your answers with your classmates.

	Agree	Disagree
1. Cheating is always wrong.	☐	☐
2. I think there is cheating in every sport.	☐	☐
3. Professional athletes are always looking for new ways to cheat.	☐	☐
4. I understand why some professional athletes cheat.	☐	☐
5. There is cheating only in professional sports.	☐	☐
6. I've seen news about professional athletes who have cheated.	☐	☐
7. Losing games on purpose for money is the worst kind of cheating.	☐	☐
8. Even if it takes time, people who cheat will always be found.	☐	☐

A Listen to the conversation and decide if the statements are T (true) or F (false).

1. The man is reading news on the Internet.   [T / F]
2. The man understands why the athlete cheated.   [T / F]
3. The man and the woman agree about cheating.   [T / F]

B Listen again and answer the comprehension questions.

1. What is the man reading?   _____

2. What does the woman think about cheating?   _____

3. What does the woman say the athlete could have done instead?   _____

C Discuss the following questions with your classmates.

1. Which person's opinion about cheating do you agree with?

2. How would you feel if you were the athlete's family?

3. What would you do if you were the athlete's teammate?

Pre-Reading

There are many cases of cheating by athletes. Rank the following examples from 1 (less serious) to 5 (most serious). Then, share your answers with your classmates.

		Example	Cheating Scale
1		A soccer player touches the ball with his/her hand and doesn't tell the referee.	1 / 2 / 3 / 4 / 5
2		An athlete from a poor family takes money from a gambler to lose a game on purpose.	1 / 2 / 3 / 4 / 5
3		An athlete takes illegal drugs for a quick recovery from an injury to help his/her team.	1 / 2 / 3 / 4 / 5

Reading 🎧 36

A Read the passage and answer the comprehension questions.

Many athletes have the **inclination** to cheat. In 1904, Fred Lorz won the gold medal for the Olympic marathon. Then, it was revealed that he used a car for more than half the race. Seventy-six years later, Rosie Ruiz took the subway in the Boston Marathon and ran less than a kilometer to "win" the race. In 1919, members of the Chicago White Sox were **exposed** for match fixing, or **scheming** to lose games on purpose, in the World Series. With sports being such a big business, athletes and teams continue to look for ways to become better and richer. Sometimes that can result in cheating.

The 1988 100-meter final is infamous because of drug use.

Cheating in sports is often **illegal** drug use which **enhances** performance. The 100-meter final at the 1988 Seoul Olympics is one of the most famous examples. Ben Johnson won in a world record time of 9.79 seconds. Within the next couple of days, drug testers found that Johnson had been using steroids. His gold medal and world record were taken

Cycling has had a big problem with performance-enhancing drugs.

away. In the years afterwards, six of the eight runners in the same race were found to be using steroids during their careers. Therefore, the 1988 100-meter final is now called "the dirtiest race in history."

Performance-enhancing drugs have also been a problem in baseball, cycling, boxing, and swimming. Even though sports test to find these drugs, athletes continue to look for newer and better drugs. Some athletes and teams believe that the risk of being exposed as cheaters is worth the chance of being a champion and making millions of dollars.

••

1. What were two different ways that runners cheated to "win" marathons in 1904 and 1980?

   _____

2. How did the Chicago White Sox cheat?

   _____

3. What happened to Ben Johnson after he was caught cheating?

   _____

B Discuss the following questions with your classmates.

1. Why do you think the two athletes cheated in the marathon?

2. Which is the worst type of cheating; cheating in a marathon, match fixing, or illegal drug use?

3. Which is better, becoming famous through cheating or not being famous after a long career?

Listening [2]

A Read the conversation and guess the meaning of the idiom.

1. Fill in the blank to complete the idiom. The illustration is a hint.

   A: Did you hear that Tom is in hot _____ now?

   B: I know. His teacher caught him cheating on
   the test and called his mom.

2. What does the idiom mean?

   a. Someone is working hard.

   b. Someone is sweating a lot.

   c. Someone is in trouble.

B Listen to another conversation and choose the best answer to complete each sentence.

1. The man and the woman are probably ____.

   a. married   **b.** teammates   **c.** reporters

2. The woman ____ match fixing.

   a. likes   **b.** understands   **c.** hates

3. To get money, the man needed to ____.

   a. win the game   **b.** boycott the game   **c.** lose the game

4. Now, the man ____ what he has done.

   a. has no problem with   **b.** feels bad about   **c.** is proud of

Writing

Describe your thoughts about cheating in sports. Then, close your textbook and tell your
classmates about it.

_____

_____

_____

_____

_____

Personalization

There are many types of penalties for cheating. Decide which penalties you would give to the cheaters below. Then, share your answers with your classmates.

	Individual Sports	**Team Sports**
Penalty 1	Can't play in the sport for a year or more	Can't participate in any games for a year or more
Penalty 2	Can play in the sport without prize money for a year	Get rid of the players who cheated
Penalty 3	Can play in the sport without prize money for two years	Change the coach
Penalty 4	Give back the prize money	Play games without fans
Penalty 5	Lose the championship	Lose their championship
Penalty 6	Can't play in the sport ever again	Pay money to the league
Penalty 7	Go to prison for a year	Sell the team to a new owner

Cheater	**Penalty**
1. A golfer won a championship, but later, his caddie reported that he moved his ball closer to the hole.	☐
2. A jockey received money from some gamblers and lost the race on purpose.	☐
3. A figure skater damaged the costume of another skater and won a championship.	☐
4. A race car driver has used a drug which increases stamina and won a race.	☐
5. A soccer player bet against his team and won money.	☐
6. All season, a basketball team has made the other team's basket higher so it is harder to score.	☐
7. A rugby team has given money to referees during the season to help them win games.	☐
8. Many players on a baseball team have used illegal baseball bats all season to help the team win a championship.	☐

Wrap-Up

Answer the questions. Then, share your answers with your classmates.

Unit 7 Professional Athletes

1. Why do you think many children want to be professional athletes?

   _____

2. What do you think most professional athletes do after they retire?

   _____

3. Why do male professional athletes generally make more money than females?

   _____

Unit 8 The Olympics

4. What do you think are the most popular Olympic sports in your country?

   _____

5. How do you feel about the host city when you watch the Olympics on TV?

   _____

6. Why are the Olympics usually held in big cities?

   _____

Unit 9 Cheating

7. What do you think is the main reason athletes cheat?

   _____

8. Should an athlete that has been caught cheating be allowed to play his/her sport again?

   _____

9. If there was an illegal drug that improved English skills, what would you do?

   _____

Cultural Differences

Because of globalization, the chance of meeting someone from another culture is high. Understanding how cultures are different can make communication smooth and enjoyable.

Unit 10 Attitude

"A nation's culture resides in the hearts and in the soul of its people."
Mahatma Gandhi

Unit 11 Communication

"The most important thing in communication is hearing what isn't said."
Peter Drucker

Unit 12 Time

"Time is the coin of your life. It is the only coin you have, and only you can determine how it will be spent."
Carl Sandburg

Unit 10 Attitude

Vocabulary

Read the sentences with the keywords. Then, choose their meanings (a–e) from the box.

1. *Star Wars* is in the science fiction **category** of movies. _____
2. There is often a **conflict** of opinions within a big group of people. _____
3. He would rather work as an **individual** than within a group. _____
4. When travelling to another country, we shouldn't **ignore** local customs. _____
5. He said he would wear a suit to the ceremony and told us to do **likewise**. _____

a. a disagreement between people or in a group of people
b. in a similar way
c. a single person or one person in a group
d. do nothing about
e. a group of similar types

70

Warm-Up

A Look at the pictures and answer the questions. Then, share your answers with your classmates.

a go to a coffee shop   b cook   c go shopping   d travel

1. Do you prefer to do these activities alone or with others?

    a. _____   b. _____

    c. _____   d. _____

2. How often do you do these activities?

    a. _____   b. _____

    c. _____   d. _____

3. What do you enjoy most when you do these activities?

    a. _____   b. _____

    c. _____   d. _____

4. What are some activities you would never want to do with others?

    _____

B Put a check (✓) in the box to agree or disagree with each statement below. Then, share your answers with your classmates.

	Agree	Disagree
1. I prefer to eat alone.	☐	☐
2. I need some time by myself every day.	☐	☐
3. I like places where there are a lot of people.	☐	☐
4. Having a few close friends is better than having many friends.	☐	☐
5. When I'm in a group, I like to be the leader.	☐	☐
6. I like to give my opinions.	☐	☐
7. I like answering questions in class.	☐	☐
8. If I disagree with someone, I'll tell them.	☐	☐

Listening [1] 🎧 39

A Listen to the conversation and decide if the statements are T (true) or F (false).

1. The woman likes shopping alone. [T / F]
2. The woman prefers to study alone. [T / F]
3. The man doesn't like studying in coffee shops. [T / F]

B Listen again and answer the comprehension questions.

1. Why is the man going shopping? _____
2. Why does the man like shopping by himself? _____
3. What does the woman like about coffee shops? _____

C Discuss the following questions with your classmates.

1. What are the benefits and drawbacks of studying with another person?
2. Where is your favorite place to study?
3. What is your favorite thing to do with many people?

Pre-Reading

Have you ever thought about cultural differences? Answer the questions. Then, share your answers with your classmates.

	Question	Answer
1	How do Japanese teachers teach English classes?	
2	How do native English speakers teach English classes?	
3	What is a negative stereotype about Japanese culture?	
4	What is a negative stereotype about American culture?	

Reading 40

A Read the passage and answer the comprehension questions.

Some cultural experts separate "culture" into two **categories**: collectivist and individualist. People from countries with collectivist cultures such as Guatemala, Pakistan, and Indonesia tend to stay away from **conflicts** and put more value on the group than the **individual**. This is because they want to work together peacefully. For example, a person may **ignore** a problem with another person because the peace within the group is more important than the problem to be fixed.

Some people avoid conflicts while others do not.

People from countries with individualist cultures such as the US, Italy, and the Netherlands tend to prefer independence. They are more likely to do things by themselves instead of doing things as a group. Therefore, they like traveling and living by themselves. Also they prefer to say what they believe, even if that creates conflicts with others.

Some cultures encourage speaking up in class more than others.

Understanding these differences can cause fewer problems in business meetings and classrooms. For example, if an American English teacher understands that many Japanese students are not used to speaking up in class, the teacher won't be so upset when no one raises a hand to give their opinions. **Likewise**, when Japanese students understand that the American English teacher wants students to volunteer, they may try to raise their hands more often. It is important to understand that each culture has different characteristics. When you speak to people from foreign countries, make sure to remember that they have their own cultures.

• •

1. What are two categories of culture, according to some cultural experts?
   _____

2. Which three countries are examples of having collectivist cultures?
   _____

3. If Japanese students understand how American English teachers work, what may they do?
   _____

B Discuss the following questions with your classmates.

1. What do you do when you have a problem with another person?

2. What are the benefits and drawbacks of living alone?

3. What do you think are other problems Japanese students may have in English classrooms?

Listening [2] 41

A Read the conversation and guess the meaning of the idiom.

1. Fill in the blank to complete the idiom. The illustration is a hint.

   A: It's a pain in the _____ to write this essay on paper.

   B: Well, our teacher doesn't like using computers. He still thinks handwriting is much better than using computers.

2. What does the idiom mean?

   a. Something is old-fashioned.

   b. Something is troublesome.

   c. Something is boring.

B Listen to another conversation and choose the best answer to complete each sentence.

1. The man and the woman are probably _____.

   a. teachers   **b.** students   **c.** parents

2. The woman thinks that _____ are not fun.

   a. writing essays   **b.** individual presentations   **c.** group presentations

3. The woman thinks _____ are lazy.

   a. quiet students   **b.** her friends   **c.** her teachers

4. The man is comfortable talking _____.

   a. with females   **b.** in class   **c.** in a small group

Writing

Describe a positive aspect of Japanese culture. Then, close your textbook and tell your classmates about it.

_____

_____

_____

_____

_____

Personalization

Everyone has some collectivist and individualist characteristics. Answer the questions below and calculate your points. Then, share your result with your classmates.

1. Your friends are deciding what to do after school. Most of them want to go shopping, but you would rather go to a café. What would you do?

    a. I would just go shopping with them.
    b. I would explain my feelings, but go shopping with them anyway.
    c. I would explain my feelings and try to convince them to go to the café with me.
    d. I would explain my feelings. If they don't agree, I would go to the café alone.

2. If one of your friends has behaved badly, what would you do?

    a. I wouldn't do anything.
    b. I would say something if it's only the two of us.
    c. I would say something even if other friends are there.
    d. I would say how I was shocked and advise him/her to stop such behavior.

3. You have a group project, but one member didn't do much work. What would you do?

    a. I wouldn't say anything.
    b. I would make a joke about how everyone didn't do the same amount of work.
    c. I would tell the member that he/she should have done more work.
    d. I would tell the teacher not to give the member the same grade as other members.

4. If you travel abroad, which plan would you choose?

    a. I would join a group tour with only travelers from my own country.
    b. I would join a group tour with a few travelers from my own country.
    c. I would join a group tour planned by a local travel agency in the country I'm visiting.
    d. I would make a plan to travel by myself.

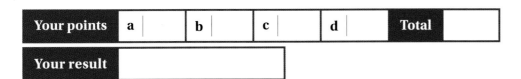

Points for each answer	a = 1	b = 2	c = 3	d = 4

Result	Individualist 16	Both 8	Collectivist 4

Your points	a	b	c	d	Total	

Your result	

Unit 11　Communication

Vocabulary

Read the sentences with the keywords. Then, choose their meanings (a–e) from the box.

1. I have never lived abroad. **Conversely**, I have traveled to over 20 countries. _____
2. Mandarin is one of the most **complex** languages in the world to learn. _____
3. When we travel to other countries, we need to **consider** their cultures. _____
4. We can learn about other cultures through **interaction** with people from around the world. _____
5. Hugging is common in **physical** cultures. _____

a. think about something carefully
b. relating to the body instead of the mind
c. meeting and communicating
d. on the other hand
e. not easy or simple

Warm-Up

A Look at the pictures and answer the questions. Then, share your answers with your classmates.

1. What are they doing in each picture?

   a. _____   b. _____

   c. _____   d. _____

2. How often do you do these things with your friends?

   a. _____   b. _____

   c. _____   d. _____

3. What do you think is the relationship in each picture?

   a. _____   b. _____

   c. _____   d. _____

4. What do you think is most important for good communication?

   _____

B Put a check (✓) in the box to agree or disagree with each statement below. Then, share your answers with your classmates.

	Agree	Disagree
1. I like meeting new people.	☐	☐
2. I enjoy talking to people from other cultures.	☐	☐
3. I want to travel to many countries in the future.	☐	☐
4. It's important to research about culture before you travel.	☐	☐
5. I've learned about cultural differences from movies.	☐	☐
6. I have a good understanding of cultural differences.	☐	☐
7. I can explain my culture to people in English.	☐	☐
8. I know some gestures from other cultures.	☐	☐

Listening [1] 43

A Listen to the conversation and decide if the statements are T (true) or F (false).

1. The man, the woman, and Sara will go shopping. [T / F]
2. The man and Sara have a class together. [T / F]
3. The man wants to go on a date with Sara. [T / F]

B Listen again and answer the comprehension questions.

1. What did Sara ask the man about? _____
2. What did the man mean by his gesture? _____
3. What does the the man's gesture mean in Korea? _____

C Discuss the following questions with your classmates.

1. What are the gestures for money and love in your culture?
2. What would you have done if you were Sara?
3. Who do you usually talk with when you have a problem?

Pre-Reading

A gesture has different meanings depending on the country. Complete the chart. Then, share your answers with your classmates.

	1	2	3	4
Gesture				
Meanings	• zero (France) • •	• hate (Iran) • •	• two (the US) • •	• bad luck (Greece) • •

Reading 44

A Read the passage and answer the comprehension questions.

Communication is important. Experts believe that it is 55% body language, 38% tone of voice, and 7% the words that you use. When we talk with others, we use both verbal and non-verbal communication. Non-verbal communication such as gestures, head movements, and facial expressions can be different between countries. For example, the thumbs-up gesture can mean "good job" or "OK" in Australia, the UK, and Canada. **Conversely**, the same gesture is thought to be rude in Latin American countries, Iran, and Afghanistan. Although gestures can seem simple, they are actually very **complex**.

Gestures can mean different things in different cultures.

Personal space is also different around the world. In countries like the UK and Mexico, people usually speak to a stranger about 90 centimeters apart. In Romania, people stand as far as 140 centimeters away, as it would be **considered** rude to stand closer. This can lead to an uncomfortable **interaction** between two people from Romania and Mexico, for instance: One person would move closer while the other would move away when talking.

Distance during communication is not the same in every culture.

The way of greeting someone is also different. Brazil is seen as a **physical** culture where people hug and touch quite often. On the other hand, the same actions could make someone uncomfortable in Germany. Even greeting someone with a kiss on the cheek is different. People in Argentina and the Philippines prefer one kiss, but people in Spain and Italy give two. When traveling abroad or meeting someone from another country, it is important to remember that cultures interact differently.

....

1. What are three examples of non-verbal communication?

_____

2. In which countries do people usually speak to a stranger about 90 centimeters apart?

_____

3. How might people in Germany feel about being hugged or touched?

_____

B Discuss the following questions with your classmates.

1. Which do you think is more important, verbal or non-verbal communication?

2. How would you feel if someone was talking to you from 140 centimeters away?

3. How would you feel if someone from your own culture hugged or kissed you?

A Read the conversation and guess the meaning of the idiom.

1. Fill in the blank to complete the idiom. The illustration is a hint.

   A: Are you joining our party tonight?

   B: I don't think so. I'm a _____ at parties.

   A: You don't have to socialize. Just enjoy the food and music.

2. What does the idiom mean?

   a. Someone who is very friendly in social situations.

   b. Someone who speaks loudly in social situations.

   c. Someone who is shy in social situations.

B Listen to another conversation and choose the best answer to complete each sentence.

1. The man and the woman are probably _____.

   a. at a park   **b.** in a tall building   **c.** at a party

2. The woman would stand about _____ meters away from a stranger.

   a. 0.5 meters   **b.** 1 meter   **c.** 1.5 meters

3. The man says that _____ doesn't feel comfortable with strangers.

   a. the woman   **b.** he   **c.** a person in an elevator

4. The woman doesn't like _____.

   a. physical contact   **b.** personal space   **c.** body language

Writing

Describe what you would do at a party where you don't know anyone. Then, close your textbook and tell your classmates about it.

_____

_____

_____

_____

Personalization

Everyone has a different level of comfort depending on the situation or relationship. Complete the information below. Then, share your answers with your classmates.

1. If I were talking to my parents, I'd probably be about _____ cm away from them.

2. With my brother(s) and sister(s), _____ cm is a comfortable distance for me.

3. When speaking with my best friend, I would stand about _____ cm away.

4. I would be around _____ cm from my classmates if I spoke to them in class.

5. When I meet someone for the first time, _____ cm is the distance I stand from them.

6. Based on the information above, my comfortable friend zone is between _____ cm and _____ cm.

7. If someone asked me for directions on the street and the person started moving closer to me while talking, I would _____
   _____
   _____ .

8. If I said goodbye to my international friend at the airport and he/she tried to kiss me on the cheek, I would _____
   _____
   _____ .

9. If I had an international partner and he/she hugged and kissed me in public often, I would _____
   _____
   _____ .

Unit 12　Time

Vocabulary 46

Read the sentences with the keywords. Then, choose their meanings (a–e) from the box.

1. His **interpretation** of being on time is different than mine. _____

2. Companies **prioritize** their new items in advertisements. _____

3. His leadership skills make him a **potential** manager. _____

4. I would **appreciate** it if you could come to the office one hour earlier tomorrow. _____

5. Some jobs put an **emphasis** on strong relationships with customers. _____

---

a. something that is given special importance or attention
b. could become something in the future
c. way of understanding something
d. rank things by how important they are
e. express feelings of thankfulness

Warm-Up

A Look at the pictures and answer the questions. Then, share your answers with your classmates.

a waiting for a doctor

b waiting for your friend

c waiting for your order

d waiting in a line

1. Where do you typically do these things?

   a. _____   b. _____

   c. _____   d. _____

2. How long can you wait in these situations?

   a. _____   b. _____

   c. _____   d. _____

3. What would you do if you couldn't wait anymore?

   a. _____   b. _____

   c. _____   d. _____

4. In what situations, would you wait for more than one hour?

   _____

B Put a check (✓) in the box to agree or disagree with each statement below. Then, share your answers with your classmates.

	Agree	Disagree
1. I'm usually on time.	☐	☐
2. I don't care if people are late for a meeting with me.	☐	☐
3. In my country, being on time is important.	☐	☐
4. I think I use my free time well.	☐	☐
5. In my culture, people have meetings often.	☐	☐
6. Meetings should always start and finish on time.	☐	☐
7. Meetings should only be held when there is important news.	☐	☐
8. There should be time to talk about casual things during meetings.	☐	☐

A Listen to the conversation and decide if the statements are T (true) or F (false).

1. The man is late to meet the woman.   [T / F]
2. The woman's family is never late.   [T / F]
3. The woman can wait in line for 45 minutes.   [T / F]

B Listen again and answer the comprehension questions.

1. Who would arrive second in the man's family? _____
2. Who would arrive last in the woman's family? _____
3. How long does the man say he can wait to eat? _____

C Discuss the following questions with your classmates.

1. How long would you wait in line for lunch when you are very hungry?
2. What is the longest time you have ever waited in line?
3. What do you usually do when you are waiting for someone or something?

Pre-Reading

In which countries or areas do you think the following happens on time or late? Complete the chart. Then, share your answers with your classmates.

	Circumstance	On Time	Late
1	Arrival/Departure of public transportation		
2	Opening a shop each day		
3	Appointments with friends		
4	Starting business meetings		
5	Finishing business meetings		

Reading 48

A Read the passage and answer the comprehension questions.

Different **interpretations** of time can lead to misunderstandings and conflicts. According to some experts, cultures can be either monochronic (M-time) or polychronic (P-time). Cultures that are M-time **prioritize** clock time, so not being late and working on one thing at a time is important. This is a **potential** problem if a person from an M-time culture is working with a person from a P-time culture. For example, a person from an M-time culture would

For some people, it is OK to be late.

expect meetings to start on time and could be upset when the P-time culture person is late. Examples of countries having mostly M-time cultures are Germany and the US.

Conversely, P-time cultures **appreciate** relationships over time, so it is normal for people in these cultures not to rush through appointments. In other words, relationships are more important than time, which can make people more than one hour late for their next appointment. For example, a P-time culture person may not understand why M-time culture people are upset when the person is late for a meeting. India, Italy, and Greece are examples of countries having mostly P-time cultures.

Countries such as Japan are actually both M-time and P-time. While most Japanese people are on time, there is also an **emphasis** on relationships and maintaining group harmony. For example, a meeting in Japan may finish later than scheduled if the group is discussing something important. This is because ending the discussion due to time would be considered rude. In conclusion, the way a person feels about time can include a variety of different factors.

· ·

1. What are two things that M-time cultures value?

    _____

2. Why do people from P-time cultures not rush through appointments?

    _____

3. What is an example of M-time culture in Japan?

    _____

B Discuss the following questions with your classmates.

1. What kinds of things do you feel are important to be on time for?
2. In what situations, do you think you can be late for an appointment?
3. Which do you think is more important, finishing things on time or trying to build relationships?

Listening [2]

A Read the conversation and guess the meaning of the idiom.

1. Fill in the blank to complete the idiom. The illustration is a hint.

   A: Should we study one more page?

   B: Well, we've just _____ out of time.
   Let's finish class now.

2. What does the idiom mean?

   a. There are a few minutes left.

   b. There is no time left.

   c. The time was wasted.

B Listen to another conversation and choose the best answer to complete each sentence.

1. The man and the woman are probably _____.

   a. co-workers   **b.** students   **c.** teachers

2. The debate club has meetings _____.

   a. every day   **b.** once a month   **c.** every Thursday

3. The teacher continued talking _____ minutes after the meeting was supposed to finish.

   a. 60   **b.** 45   **c.** 30

4. The teacher thinks talking _____ is important for good relationships.

   a. with each other   **b.** about global issues   **c.** about debate rules

Writing

Describe an experience when you were late for something. Then, close your textbook and tell your classmates about it.

_____

_____

_____

_____

_____

Food and Health

Technology

Sports

Cultural Differences

Society

Personalization

There are many factors to being M-time or P-time. Answer the questions below and calculate your points. Then, share your result with your classmates.

1. How many things do you usually do at once?

   a. I do one thing at a time.   **b.** It depends.   **c.** I do more than one thing at a time.

2. When you are doing something, can you stay focused on what you are doing?

   a. Yes, I can focus.   **b.** It depends.   **c.** No, I can't focus.

3. When you work on something, which is more important, finishing or learning?

   a. I just want to finish it.   **b.** It depends.   **c.** I want to learn something while I do it.

4. Once you make a certain plan, do you stay with it?

   a. Yes, I usually follow it.   **b.** It depends.   **c.** No, I usually change it.

5. When you meet someone, do you arrive on time?

   a. Yes, I'm always on time.   **b.** It depends.   **c.** No, I'm always late.

6. When you are working in a group, which is more important, working together or just finishing it?

   a. I just want to finish.   **b.** It depends.   **c.** I think teamwork is important.

7. Which idiom is similar to how you think about time, "time flies" or "time is money"?

   a. I prefer "time is money."   **b.** It depends.   **c.** I prefer "time flies."

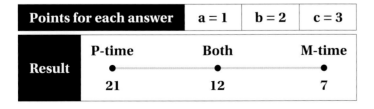

Points for each answer	a = 1	b = 2	c = 3

Result	P-time	Both	M-time
	21	12	7

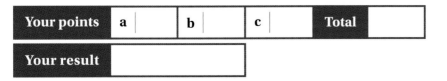

Your points	a	b	c	Total	
Your result					

Wrap-Up

Answer the questions. Then, share your answers with your classmates.

Unit 10 Attitude

1. In a classroom, what are the benefits and drawbacks of doing pair work?

   _____

2. Would you rather live in a country that is collectivist or individualist?

   _____

3. In what situations, do you think it is better to ignore a problem rather than try to fix it?

   _____

Unit 11 Communication

4. What gestures do you make when you say no?

   _____

5. What topics are good to talk about when meeting someone for the first time?

   _____

6. What behaviors are considered rude in your country?

   _____

Unit 12 Time

7. What causes you to lose focus when working on a task?

   _____

8. Would you rather have one long meeting once a month or several short meetings in a month?

   _____

9. If you were the leader of a group, what rules would you make for your meetings?

   _____

Society

We are all a part of society regardless of where we live.
However, every society around the world faces social issues differently.

Unit 13 Education
"He who opens a school door, closes a prison."
Victor Hugo

Unit 14 Immigration
"Our immigration policy should be based on compassion and a desire to help the other."
Ilhan Omar

Unit 15 Gender Differences
"A gender-equal society would be one where the word 'gender' does not exist: where anyone can be themselves."
Gloria Steinem

Unit 13 — Education

Vocabulary

Read the sentences with the keywords. Then, choose their meanings (a–e) from the box.

1. This year is **significant** because we'll graduate from school. _____

2. If you keep practicing, **eventually** your skills will get better. _____

3. Since the **environment** in this classroom is good, we can enjoy studying. _____

4. We are **required** to take at least five English classes before we graduate. _____

5. Since the Spanish and Portuguese languages are **similar**, I sometimes mix them up. _____

> a. very important
> b. have to do something
> c. the conditions or situations around something or someone
> d. almost the same
> e. after some time

Warm-Up

A Look at the pictures and answer the questions. Then, share your answers with your classmates.

class

lunch

sports day

club

1. What are your best memories of these school activities?

   a. _____   b. _____

   c. _____   d. _____

2. What did you not like about these school activities?

   a. _____   b. _____

   c. _____   d. _____

3. If you were a teacher, what would you want your students to learn through these activities?

   a. _____   b. _____

   c. _____   d. _____

4. What subjects did you enjoy most in school?

   _____

B Put a check (✓) in the box to agree or disagree with each statement below. Then, share your answers with your classmates.

	Agree	Disagree
1. I've had a good education.	☐	☐
2. I've had very good teachers.	☐	☐
3. I'm good at taking tests.	☐	☐
4. Education is the most important thing if you want to be successful.	☐	☐
5. Students in my country have to study a lot.	☐	☐
6. The university entrance examination system in my country is good.	☐	☐
7. The name of the university you graduate from is important.	☐	☐
8. The skills you get at university will help you in your future job.	☐	☐

Listening [1] 51

A Listen to the conversation and decide if the statements are T (true) or F (false).

1. The man and the woman went to the same high school. [T / F]
2. The woman didn't like her high school. [T / F]
3. The man went to a co-ed school. [T / F]

B Listen again and answer the comprehension questions.

1. Who wanted the woman to go to the all-girls high school? _____
2. What did the man and his friends like doing more than studying? _____
3. Who bothered the woman when she was studying? _____

C Discuss the following questions with your classmates.

1. In the future, would you want your children to go to the same schools that you did?
2. What are the benefits and drawbacks of going to an all-boys or all-girls school?
3. How would things be different if you had gone to a different high school?

Pre-Reading

Have you ever thought about the importance of education? Answer the questions. Then, share your answers with your classmates.

	Question	Answer
1	What are the good points of your country's education system?	
2	What are the bad points of your country's education system?	
3	Which countries do you think have a good education system?	
4	What are the qualities of a good teacher?	

Reading 52

A Read the passage and answer the comprehension questions.

Education is a **significant** factor in a person's success. By studying hard, you can do well in high school which will help your admission into a good university, and **eventually**, you can have a successful job. Every country's education system is different, and learning **environments** are not equal around the world.

One of the reasons why education quality is low in South Africa is poorly trained teachers.

Finland's education system is among the best in the world, led by the belief "Less is more." Children do not begin school until they are seven years old and the school day is about five-hours long. Additionally, students are rarely tested or given homework before the age of 16. In other words, Finnish people focus on social intelligence rather than academic intelligence. Another key to Finland's system is high teacher quality: All teachers are **required** to have a master's degree. However, only the top 10% of university graduates can enter the teaching course.

Unfortunately, not all children around the world have the chance to succeed academically. South Africa, for example, has a large gap between the highest- and lowest-level schools. The curriculums for its highest-level schools are **similar** to the best schools in Singapore, the UK, and the US. In contrast, other schools in the country have curriculums that are among the lowest of all developing countries. A big reason is low teacher quality. In one study, math teachers took the same test given to their students and 79% of them scored below the standard level. This means that most of the teachers didn't know how to do the math that they were teaching their students. Sadly, problems like this, and worse, are found in many education systems around the world.

••

1. How long is the school day in Finland?

   _____

2. Who can enter the teaching course in Finland?

   _____

3. What is a reason some South African schools have low-level curriculums?

   _____

B Discuss the following questions with your classmates.

1. What does it mean to do well in high school?

2. Do you think Finland's school system would be successful in your country?

3. Which is more important, social intelligence or academic intelligence?

Listening [2]

A Read the conversation and guess the meaning of the idiom.

1. Fill in the blank to complete the idiom. The illustration is a hint.

   A: I'm traveling next month, so I should find another part-time job.

   B: I'm in the same _____. I need money for a new car.

2. What does the idiom mean?

   a. Someone has a similar job as others.

   b. Someone has a similar travel plan as others.

   c. Someone has a similar problem as others.

B Listen to another conversation and choose the best answer to complete each sentence.

1. The man and the woman are probably _____.

   a. cooks   **b.** students   **c.** teachers

2. The man says that South Korean students are like French students because they also _____.

   a. are taught to enjoy mealtimes   **b.** take one-to-two hour lunches   **c.** use cloth napkins

3. In France, students eat _____ at least once a week.

   a. with their teachers   **b.** in a restaurant   **c.** a vegetarian meal

4. The man and the woman can't have lunch yet because they _____.

   a. are on the boat   **b.** are on a diet   **c.** have things to do

Writing

Describe why university education should be free of charge. Then, close your textbook and tell your classmates about it.

_____

_____

_____

_____

_____

Food and Health

Technology

Sports

Cultural Differences

Society

Personalization

There are many factors which lead to a good education. Rank the following factors from 1 (less important) to 5 (very important). Then, share your answers with your classmates.

Factor	Importance
1. Having supportive family members	[1 / 2 / 3 / 4 / 5]
2. Having highly trained teachers	[1 / 2 / 3 / 4 / 5]
3. Having the financial support of the government	[1 / 2 / 3 / 4 / 5]
4. Doing a lot of homework	[1 / 2 / 3 / 4 / 5]
5. Having nice school facilities	[1 / 2 / 3 / 4 / 5]
6. Being in a good location	[1 / 2 / 3 / 4 / 5]
7. Having supportive friends	[1 / 2 / 3 / 4 / 5]

Unit 14 **Immigration**

Vocabulary

Read the sentences with the keywords. Then, choose their meanings (a–e) from the box.

1. The **expansion** of refugee camps was caused by a large number of immigrants. _____
2. Although he was a **resident** of Tokyo for three years, he didn't learn to speak Japanese. _____
3. My **integration** was smooth because there were many people from my country here. _____
4. There is a **community** of volunteers to help immigrants live in our city. _____
5. In this class, there are many **ethnic** backgrounds such as European and South American. _____

a. the action of making someone or something a part of a larger group
b. a person who lives in a place
c. a group of people living in one area
d. the action of getting bigger
e. about a group of people with common cultures such as customs and beliefs

Warm-Up

A Look at the pictures and answer the questions. Then, share your answers with your classmates.

1. What are the names of these multicultural cities and countries?

   a. _____   b. _____

   c. _____   d. _____

2. What language is mainly spoken in each country?

   a. _____   b. _____

   c. _____   d. _____

3. What immigrant groups are common in each country?

   a. _____   b. _____

   c. _____   d. _____

4. What immigrant groups are common in your country?

   _____

B Put a check (✓) in the box to agree or disagree with each statement below. Then, share your answers with your classmates.

	Agree	Disagree
1. My city is multicultural.	☐	☐
2. I never want to live in another country.	☐	☐
3. My country has many immigrants.	☐	☐
4. Recently, I think the number of immigrants in my country is increasing.	☐	☐
5. I try to help people who can't communicate in my country's language.	☐	☐
6. If you live in a foreign country, you must master that country's language.	☐	☐
7. I want to work for a company with people from many different countries.	☐	☐
8. I want to work for a boss that is from the same country as me.	☐	☐

Listening [1] 55

A Listen to the conversation and decide if the statements are T (true) or F (false).

1. The man was born in the US.   [T / F]
2. The man has two sisters.   [T / F]
3. The man's parents run three diners now.   [T / F]

B Listen again and answer the comprehension questions.

1. Which country is the man's family from?   _____
2. What was the man's parents' previous job?   _____
3. What did the first customer leave on the table?   _____

C Discuss the following questions with your classmates.

1. Which do you think is more difficult to learn, language or culture?
2. If you could move to another country, which country would you choose?
3. What kind of work could you do if you lived overseas?

Pre-Reading

You have culture shock when you feel stress from new situations in a different culture. Match the four stages of culture shock with their meanings (a–d). Then, discuss the following questions with your classmates.

Stage 1 The honeymoon stage   _____

Stage 2 The anxiety stage   _____

Stage 3 The adjustment stage   _____

Stage 4 The acceptance stage   _____

   a. As language skills improve, it is easier to communicate.

   b. As you learn the culture, you start to feel at home.

   c. Stress from a new place, makes it difficult to communicate.

   d. Everything is new, exciting, and fun. It is like taking a vacation.

1. What are some things you can do to avoid feeling culture shock?

2. What do you think is the most difficult part of moving to another country?

Reading 56

A Read the passage and answer the comprehension questions.

The **expansion** of immigration around the world has both positives and negatives. Some people are against immigration because they feel immigrants are taking jobs away from local **residents**. However, many immigrants take work that local residents prefer not to take, such as factory, agricultural, and cleaning work. Without those workers, a country's production rate can go down and have a negative impact on the economy.

In some countries, immigrants do much of the agricultural work.

Another factor is the **integration** of immigrants into their new country. Some people think that immigrants do not try to adapt into their new country and only spend time with other immigrants. As a result, instead of big multicultural **communities**, small split communities are made up. For example, many Koreans spend their time in Koreatown in Los Angeles. Although LA is culturally diverse, Koreatown is made up of shops and restaurants with Korean owners. This type of small **ethnic** neighborhood is found in France, the UK, and Germany as well.

There is a large Turkish community in Germany.

Sometimes, the problem with immigration is caused by a country's government. In Japan, a politician once said that Japan was "one culture, one civilization, one language, and one ethnic group." Many people disagreed with this idea. Now, the number of non-Japanese citizens has slowly been increasing. Many experts believe that some problems of the aging society can be solved by allowing more immigrants into Japan. Immigration can be a positive for a country and its economy. Therefore, it is important to have a community which is supportive of immigrants.

....

1. What are some examples of work that immigrants do?

   _____

2. What do some immigrants do instead of trying to adapt to their new country?

   _____

3. What can Japan solve by allowing more immigrants?

   _____

B Discuss the following questions with your classmates.

1. What kind of work do immigrants usually do in your country?

2. What kinds of split communities are there in your country?

3. How can a government help immigrants adapt to their new country?

Listening [2] 57

A Read the conversation and guess the meaning of the idiom.

1. Fill in the blank to complete the idiom. The illustration is a hint.

    A: My parents and I are scientists, but my brother didn't even finish high school. He used to be the _____ sheep in our family.

    B: Not anymore. He is a famous artist now! Isn't that great?

2. What does the idiom mean?

    a. Someone who is better than everyone else.

    b. Someone who is always alone.

    c. Someone who is odd or different from everyone else.

B Listen to another conversation and choose the best answer to complete each sentence.

1. The man and the woman are probably _____.

    a. brother and sister   **b.** father and daughter   **c.** husband and wife

2. The man's parents didn't talk to him for a while because he _____.

    a. left China   **b.** didn't have a job   **c.** had no money

3. The man lives _____ now.

    a. in China   **b.** alone   **c.** with the woman

4. The woman will probably _____ soon.

    a. move back home   **b.** start working in the US   **c.** go to a graduate school

Writing

Describe what you would do to help an immigrant family that moved into your neighborhood. Then, close your textbook and tell your classmates about it.

_____

_____

_____

_____

_____

Personalization

There are many different views on immigration and living in a foreign country. Decide if you agree or disagree with the statements below and write reasons. Then, share your answers with your classmates.

Statement	Agree / Disagree
1.  My country would lose its culture if it accepted more immigrants.	
2.  Allowing more immigrants would help the economy.	
3.  Crime will increase if more immigrants are allowed to enter the country.	
4.  My country would benefit by becoming more culturally diverse with increased immigration.	
5.  It would be easy for an immigrant to adapt to living in my country.	
6.  When a person moves to a new country, he/she shouldn't be friends with people from his/her own culture.	
7.  If you were at the anxiety stage of culutre shock, you should study language harder to move to the adjustment stage.	

Unit 15   Gender Differences

Vocabulary

Read the sentences with the keywords. Then, choose their meanings (a–e) from the box.

1. It was a **radical** idea for the airline to hire only female pilots. _____
2. Since he is so active and she is so lazy, there is a **contrast** in their characters. _____
3. If men and women both **participate** in the debate, we may have a bigger range of opinions. _____
4. Having a female president can **affect** the government in a positive way. _____
5. The small number of women in government has **motivated** her to become Prime Minster. _____

a. difference between people or things
b. join in an activity or event
c. be the reason for wanting to do something
d. very different from what is normal
e. have an impact on someone or something

Warm-Up

A Look at the pictures and answer the questions. Then, share your answers with your classmates.

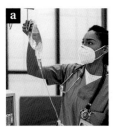    

1. What is the name of the job in each picture?

   a. _____   b. _____   c. _____

   d. _____   e. _____

2. Do you think these jobs are usually done by men or women?

   a. _____   b. _____   c. _____

   d. _____   e. _____

3. What kinds of personalities do you think are suitable for these jobs?

   a. _____   b. _____   c. _____

   d. _____   e. _____

4. What is the biggest difference between males and females?

   _____

B Put a check (✓) in the box to agree or disagree with each statement below. Then, share your answers with your classmates.

	Agree	Disagree
1. I think the mother should be the main person taking care of a child.	☐	☐
2. I think a husband and wife should do the cooking together.	☐	☐
3. I prefer to communicate with someone who is the same gender as me.	☐	☐
4. I'd rather have a teacher who is the same gender as me.	☐	☐
5. I prefer to work for a boss who is the same gender as me.	☐	☐
6. I'd rather see a doctor who is the same gender as me.	☐	☐
7. My country has many women as company presidents.	☐	☐
8. My country has many women in the government.	☐	☐

Listening [1]

A Listen to the conversation and decide if the statements are T (true) or F (false).

1. The woman is talking about a video that she watched.   [T / F]
2. The woman's father likes talking about music.   [T / F]
3. The woman watches baseball with her father.   [T / F]

B Listen again and answer the comprehension questions.

1. Who talks more between the man and the woman?   _____
2. What topics does the woman's mother prefer?   _____
3. Who cooks dinner in the woman's family?   _____

C Discuss the following questions with your classmates.

1. Among your friends, who tends to talk more, males or females?
2. What different topics do you talk about with your male and female friends?
3. What do you usually talk about with your parents?

Pre-Reading

What are your views on the differences in gender? Decide if you agree or disagree with the statements below and write reasons. Then, share your answers with your classmates.

	Statement	Agree / Disagree
1	Women go shopping because they enjoy it, while men go shopping because they need to buy something.	
2	Men want to finish shopping quickly, but women enjoy visiting many stores.	
3	Women make shopping decisions depending on how they feel, while men make shopping decisions based on data and facts.	
4	Men buy things because of brand, but women buy things because of friendly service and relationships with the shop staff.	

Reading 60

A Read the passage and answer the comprehension questions.

The famous book, *Men Are from Mars, Women Are from Venus* states that men and women must be from two separate planets because they are so different. That may be a **radical** and simple way to look at gender differences, but there are still **contrasts** between males and females.

Some of the differences in gender may be revealed in the way males and females communicate. Non-verbally, the average woman may prefer direct eye contact, while the average man may prefer to face a person at an angle. Verbally, average males may tend to use more direct language and interrupt conversations. Conversely, average females may tend to pause more in conversations, and encourage other people to speak.

Other reasons for differences in genders can be a result of how children have been raised. Traditionally, boys have more often **participated** in sports, while girls have been involved in "process play" or "relationship play." This could possibly shape their character and **affect** the future of how they might act as men and women in the workplace. If they have been encouraged to play house or nurse, girls may learn to work together and share ideas by listening to each other. On the other hand, if boys have been **motivated** to win, they may be more assertive or aggressive. The impact of these childhood experiences can lead to people having different opinions on how to do things. Understanding such differences and tendencies in genders can lead to less conflict and better relationships between men and women.

Males and females may differ in non-verbal communication.

Playing house may teach girls how to work well with others.

•••

1. What non-verbal way may women prefer when they communicate?

   _____

2. What may average males do when they communicate verbally?

   _____

3. What kind of play have girls been traditionally involved in?

   _____

B Discuss the following questions with your classmates.

1. Which verbal and non-verbal communication style do you use?
2. When you were a child, what kinds of things did you like to do?
3. What are some sports which are more popular with females than males?

A Read the conversation and guess the meaning of the idiom.

1. Fill in the blank to complete the idiom. The illustration is a hint.

   A: Do you remember we're seeing a movie on Saturday?

   B: Oh, I forgot! My parents are visiting me this weekend.
   Can I take a _____ check. How about next weekend?

2. What does the idiom mean?

   a. Someone wants to do something later, not now.
   b. Someone doesn't want to do something in the rain.
   c. Someone wants to do something different.

B Listen to another conversation and choose the best answer to complete each sentence.

1. The man and the woman are probably _____.

   a. at a restaurant   **b.** in an office building   **c.** at a hospital

2. The woman has been away for _____.

   a. a couple of weeks   **b.** three months   **c.** a year

3. The woman can't go to the curry restaurant today because she _____.

   a. has many meetings   **b.** doesn't like the rain   **c.** had a big breakfast

4. The woman hasn't _____ the new manager yet.

   a. emailed   **b.** heard about   **c.** met

Writing

Describe how your country would be different if most of the government was female. Then, close your textbook and tell your classmates about it.

_____

_____

_____

_____

_____

Personalization

Everyone has their own views on the differences in gender. Answer the questions below. Then, share your answers with your classmates.

---

1. You are in a toy store with your son. He wants a girl doll. What would you do?

   a. I would buy the girl doll for him.

   b. I would tell him that he needs to choose something else.

   c. First, I would ask him why he wants a girl doll.

2. You have a daughter who is about to start elementary school. Which kind of school would you send her to?

   a. I would send her to a co-ed school.

   b. I would send her to an all-girls school.

   c. First, I would ask her which school she wants to go to.

3. You have a son who is about to start elementary school. Which kind of school would you send him to?

   a. I would send him to a co-ed school.

   b. I would send him to an all-boys school.

   c. First, I would ask him which school he wants to go to.

4. Your daughter wants to play soccer, but her school only has a boys' team. What would you do?

   a. I would let her play on the boys' team.

   b. I would tell her to choose another sport with a girls' team.

   c. I would try to find another school with a girls' team.

5. Your friend's wife has just given birth to a child. He has told you that he is going to quit his job to raise the child. What would you tell him?

   a. I would tell him that he has made the right choice.

   b. I would tell him that he shouldn't quit his job.

   c. I would tell him to talk with his wife about what's best for his family.

Wrap-Up

Answer the questions. Then, share your answers with your classmates.

Unit 13	Education

1. What are some of the benefits and drawbacks of school uniforms?

2. What are some differences between private and public schools?

3. What are some important factors in deciding which university to go to?

Unit 14	Immigration

4. What would be the benefits and drawbacks of having more immigrants in your community?

5. How long should immigrants live in a country before they can become citizens there?

6. Do you think your country should have refugee camps?

Unit 15	Gender Differences

7. What are some countries that you think have good or poor gender balance?

8. How are sons and daughters treated differently by their parents in your country?

9. Why do you think men often make more money than women for doing the same job?

Keywords List

Photo Credits:

cover: © Education Images/Universal Images Group/Getty Images; 9: © JillWellington/Pixabay; 10: © Pixabay or Pixels; 11: (a) © Shaiith/iStock/Getty Images Plus/Getty Images, (b) © Fudio/iStock/Getty Images Plus/Getty Images, (c) © Ryutaro Tsukata/Pixels, (d) © StockSolutions/iStock /Getty Images Plus/Getty Images; 12: © UsuHeo/Pixabay; 13: (t to b) © Quangpraha/Pixabay, © dougm56/Pixabay; 15: (1) © lloorraa/Pixabay, (2) © ROMAN ODINTSOV/Pixels, (3) © martinhosmart/iStock/Getty Images Plus/Getty Images, (4) © Roxiller/iStock/Getty Images Plus/Getty Images, (5) © xijian/E+/Getty Images, (6) © skynesher/E+/Getty Images, (7) © Ladykylie/iStock/Getty Images Plus/Getty Images, (8) © kuppa_rock/iStock /Getty Images Plus/Getty Images; 16: © Busà Photography/Moment/Getty Images; 17: (a) © SOPA Images/LightRocket/Getty Images, (b) © Tetra images/ Getty Images, (c) © IDC/ amana images/Getty Images, (d) © okimo/iStock/Getty Images Plus/Getty Images; 18: © mesut zengin/iStock /Getty Images Plus/Getty Images; 19: (t to b) © Pixabay or Pixels, © kuppa_rock iStock/Getty Images Plus/Getty Images; 21: (l to r) © bhofack2/iStock/Getty Images Plus/Getty Images, © Maria_Lapina/iStock/Getty Images Plus/Getty Images, © Tetiana_Chudovska/iStock/Getty Images Plus/Getty Images; 22: © skynesher/E+/Getty Images; 23: (a) © mikkelwilliam/E+/Getty Images, (b) © Sonia Parra/EyeEm/Getty Images, (c) © franckreporter/E+/Getty Images, (d) © Donald Miralle/Getty Images Sport/Getty Images; 24: (t to b) © Europa Press News/Europa Press/Getty Images, © AlonzoDesign/DigitalVision Vectors/Getty Images; 25: (t to b) © Michael Greenberg/DigitalVision/Getty Images, © MediaNews Group/Getty Images; 27: (t to b) © Masahiro Makino/Moment/Getty Images, © Hinterhaus Productions/DigitalVision/Getty Images, © Feifei Cui-Paoluzzo/Moment/Getty Images, © Rusty Hill/ Photodisc/Getty Images, © Jimmy Nilsson/ EyeEm/Getty Images, © kajakiki/E+/Getty Images; 29: © Yuichiro Chino/Moment/Getty Images; 30: © eclipse_images/E+/Getty Images; 31: (a) © Westend61/Getty Images, (b) © izusek/E+/Getty Images, (c) © Eric Hirata, (d) © Getty Images/The Image Bank/Getty Images; 32: © visualspace/E+/Getty Images; 33: (t to b) © picture alliance/Getty Images, © Patrick Lux/Getty Images News/Getty Images; 36: © JGI/Jamie Grill/Tetra images/Getty Images; 37: (a) © skynesher/E+/Getty Images, (b) © Mayur Kakade/Moment/Getty Images, (c) © ferrantraite/E+/Getty Images, (d) © Drazen Zigic/iStock/Getty Images Plus/Getty Images; 38: © FluxFactory/E+/Getty Images; 39: (t to b) © Klaus Vedfelt/DigitalVision/Getty Images, © PhotoAlto/Dinoco Greco/Getty Images; 41: (1) © Geber86/E+/Getty Images, (2) © Craig Ferguson/LightRocket/ Getty Images, (3) © View Pictures/Universal Images Group/Getty Images, (4) © Klaus Vedfelt/DigitalVision/Getty Images, (5) © AleksandarNakic/E+/ Getty Images, (6) © monkeybusinessimages/iStock/Getty Images Plus; 42: © onurdongel/E+/Getty Images; 43: (a) © WikimediaImages/Pixabay, (b) © De Agostini/Getty Images, (c) © Future Publishing/Future/Getty Images, (d) © Science & Society Picture Library/Getty Images; 44: © Comstock Images/Stockbyte/Getty Images, (1) © Alexander Koerner/Getty Images Europe/Getty Images, (2) © James Leynse/Corbis Historical/Getty Images, (3) © Smith Collection/Gado/Archive Photos/Getty Images; 45: (t to b) © hocus-focus/iStock Unreleased/Getty Images, © picture alliance/Getty Images; 47: (1) © TOBIAS SCHWARZ/AFP/Getty Images, (2) © TOSHIFUMI KITAMURA/AFP/Getty Images, (3) © Donald Iain Smith/Tetra images/Getty Images, (4) © China News Service/Getty Images, (5) © gerenme/iStock/Getty Images Plus, (6) © gorodenkoff/iStock/Getty Images Plus, (7) © Paul Souders/Stone/Getty Images; 49: © Dmytro Aksonov/E+/Getty Images; 50: © G Fiume/Getty Images Sport/Getty Images; 51: (a) © DeFodi Images/ Getty Images, (b) © MediaNews Group/Orange County Register via Getty Images/Getty Images, (c) © SOPA Images/LightRocket/Getty Images, (d) © G Fiume/Getty Images Sport/Getty Images; 52: © Eric Hirata, (t to b, l to r) © Westend61/Getty Images, © Bradley Kanaris/Getty Images Sport/Getty Images, © Morsa Images/DigitalVision/Getty Images, © TOLGA AKMEN/AFP/Getty Images, © imcockpit/Pixabay, © NurPhoto/Getty Images, © Europa Press News/Getty Images, © Blend Images - Stretch Photography/Tetra images/Getty Images ; 53: (t to b) © Harriet Lander/Copa/Getty Images Sport/Getty Images, © TIMOTHY A. CLARY/AFP/Getty Images; 55: (1) © Martyn Lucy/Getty Images Sport/Getty Images, (2) © Zak Hussein - PA Images/Getty Images, (3) © SIA KAMBOU/AFP/Getty Images, (4) © ZhangKun/Moment/Getty Images, (5) © Mark Reinstein/Corbis Historical/ Getty Images, (6) © JamesBrey /E+/Getty Images , (7) © Jim McIsaac/Getty Images Sport/Getty Images; 56: © Rob Carr/Getty Images Sport/Getty Images; 57: (a) © BSR Agency/Getty Images Sport/Getty Images, (b) © LILLIAN SUWANRUMPHA/AFP/Getty Images, (c) © Clive Brunskill/Getty Images Sport/Getty Images, (d) © picture alliance/Getty Images; 58: © Jamie Squire/Getty Images Sport/Getty Images; 59: (t to b) © Visual China Group/ Getty Images, © NCAA Photos/Getty Images; 61: (1) © Jonathan Ferrey/Getty Images Sport/Getty Images, (2) © Buda Mendes/Getty Images Sport/ Getty Images, (3) © NurPhoto/Getty Images, (4) © Patrick Smith/Getty Images Sport/Getty Images, (5) © TEH ENG KOON/AFP/Getty Images, (6) © Jeff Greenberg/Universal Images Group/Getty Images, (7) © South China Morning Post/Getty Images; 62: © NurPhoto/Getty Images; 63: (a) © NurPhoto/Getty Image, (b) © Europa Press Sports/Getty Images, (c) © Markus Tobisch/Getty Images Sport/Getty Images, (d) © Hagen Hopkins/ Getty Images Sport/Getty Images; 64: © Valeriy_G/iStock/Getty Images Plus/Getty Images, (1) © 134213/Pixabay, (2) © Ngampol Thongsai/EyeEm/ Getty Images, (3) © Motortion/   iStock/Getty Images Plus/Getty Images ; 65: (t to b) © Bettmann/Getty Images, © Dario Belingheri/Velo/Getty Images; 67: (l to r) © Fuse/Corbis/Getty Images, © Patrik Giardino/Corbis/Getty Images, © stevecoleimages/E+/Getty Images, © Photo by Alex Gaidouk/Moment/Getty Images; 69: © Kyodo News/Getty Images; 70: © Tim Graham/Getty Images News/Getty Images; 71: (a) © AJ_Watt/E+/Getty Images, (b) © Moyo Studio/E+/Getty Images, (c) © Gideon Mendel/Corbis News/Getty Images, (d) © SolStock/E+/Getty Images; 72: © leventince/E+/ Getty Images; 73: (t to b) © Westend61/Getty Images, © skynesher/E+/Getty Images; 76: © Yue_/E+/Getty Images; 77: (a) © miljko/E+/Getty Images, (b) © Westend61/Getty Images, (c) © Superb Images/The Image Bank/Getty Images, (d) © Dreet Production/Cavan/Getty Images; 78: © justocker/ iStock/Getty Images Plus/Getty Images, (1) © Christian Adams/The Image Bank/Getty Images, (2) © Christian Adams/The Image Bank/Getty Images, (3) © Christian Adams/The Image Bank/Getty Images, (4) © borisyankov/ E+ /Getty Images; 79: (t to b) © DAMIEN MEYER/AFP/Getty Images, © AFP/ Getty Images; 81: (t to b) © monkeybusinessimages/ iStock/Getty Images Plus/Getty Images, © LeoPatrizi/E+/Getty Images, © Hinterhaus Productions/DigitalVision /Getty Images, © Halfpoint Images/Moment/Getty Images, © PHOTO MIO JAPAN/DigitalVision/Getty Images, © portishead1/E+/Getty Images, © YakobchukOlena/iStock/Getty Images Plus/Getty Images, © Alexander Spatari/Moment/Getty Images; 82: © Travelpix Ltd/Stone/Getty Imges; 83: (a) © Thomas Barwick/DigitalVision/Getty Images, (b) © Tomas Rodriguez/Stone/Getty Images, (c) © Vladimir Vladimirov/E+/Getty Images, (d) © TkKurikawa/iStock Editorial/Getty Images Plus/Getty Images; 84: © Michal Stipek/iStock Editorial/Getty Images Plus/Getty Images; 85: © Majority World/Universal Images Group/Getty Images; 89: © Orbon Alija/E+/Getty Images; 90: © marcela_net/Pixabay; 91: (a) © urbancow/E+/Getty Images, (b) © Delly Carr/Getty Images Sport/Getty Images, (c) © Eric Hirata, (d) © JGalione/E+/Getty Images; 92: © D76MasahiroIKEDA/E+/Getty Images; 93: © Alain Nogues/Sygma/Getty Images; 95: (1) © Justin Paget/DigitalVision/Getty Images, (2) © Igor Alecsander/iStock/Getty Images Plus/Getty Images, (3) © Nerthuz/iStock/Getty Images Plus/Getty Images, (4) © Dougal Waters/DigitalVision/Getty Images, (5) © View Pictures/Universal Images Group/Getty Images, (6) © Bildagentur-online/Universal Images Group/Getty Images, (7) © Marko Geber/DigitalVision/Getty Images; 96: © Gideon Mendel/Corbis Historical/Getty Images; 97: (a) © lupengyu/Moment/Getty Images, (b) © TangMan Photography/Moment/Getty Images, (c) © joe daniel price/Moment/Getty Images, (d) © OlegAlbinsky/iStock/Getty Images Plus/Getty Images; 98: © Portland Press Herald/Getty Images; 99: (t to b) © Andrew Lichtenstein/Corbis Historical/Getty Images, © ullstein bild/Getty Images; 101: (1) © AHMED OUOBA/AFP/Getty Images, (2) © SEBASTIEN BOZON/AFP/Getty Images, (3) © SAUL LOEB/AFP/Getty Images, (4) © Brook Mitchell/Getty Images News/Getty Images, (5) © KAZUHIRO NOGI/AFP/Getty Images, (6) © NurPhoto/Getty Images, (7) © Carsten Koall/Getty Images News/Getty Images; 102: © Zave Smith/Stone/Getty Imges; 103: (a) © andresr/E+/Getty Images, (b) © Richard Drury/Stone/Getty Images, (c) © DigtialStorm/ iStock/Getty Images Plus/Getty Images, (d) © avid_creative/E+/Getty Images, (e) © CasarsaGuru/E+/Getty Images; 104: © Carlos M. Saavedra/Sports Illustrated/Getty Images; 105: (t to b) © Luis Alvarez/DigitalVision/Getty Images, © Cavan Images/Getty Images; 107: (1) © picture alliance/Getty Images, (2) © maroke/iStock/Getty Images Plus/Getty Images, (3) © Indeed/ABSODELS/Getty Images, (4) © Patrik Giardino/Stone/Getty Images, (5) © UFO RF/amana images/Getty Images

クラス用音声CD有り(別売)

Vantage Point
―Enhancing Communication Skills through High-Interest Topics

2023年3月1日　初版発行

著　者　Eric Hirata
発行者　松村達生
発行所　センゲージ ラーニング株式会社
　　　　〒102-0073　東京都千代田区九段北1-11-11　第2フナトビル5階
　　　　電話 03-3511-4392　FAX 03-3511-4391
　　　　e-mail: eltjapan@cengage.com
　　　　copyright©2023 センゲージ ラーニング株式会社

装　丁　　足立友幸(parastyle inc.)
編集協力　飯尾緑子(parastyle inc.)
イラスト　大塚砂織
印刷・製本　株式会社ムレコミュニケーションズ

ISBN 978-4-86312-403-5